THE ESSEN

The Essential Dublin

COMPILED AND EDITED BY
TERRY KELLEHER

GILL AND MACMILLAN

First published in 1972

Gill and Macmillan Limited
2 Belvedere Place
Dublin 1
and in London through association with the
Macmillan
Group of Publishing Companies

Cover designed by Des McCarthy

7171 0584 9

Printing history
10 9 8 7 6 5 4 3 2 1

Printed and bound in the Republic of Ireland by
Cahill and Company Limited Dublin

CONTENTS

5

7

INTRODUCTION

THERE are many facts and comments included in this book which would not find their way into a conventional tourist guide, but then it was not my intention to write a book for tourists. For *visitors* to Dublin, yes, but not for tourists. The distinction is more than academic; it is not a matter of length of stay or type of travel, but a question of attitude. The tourist expects and accepts a projected image of a place, the visitor looks for something more. He attempts to see a place through the eyes of the inhabitants, and like the inhabitants of Dublin he will have to share the problems of urbanisation, traffic jams, crowds, bureaucracy and an increasing number of rules, regulations and limitations. And so this book is also intended to be of use to Dubliners themselves.

Dublin does not offer the excitement of London, the mystery of Istanbul, the splendour of Paris or the sheer physical presence of New York, but it *does* have an atmosphere, a way of life, which is equally unique and attractive. This quality cannot be discovered or experienced through the pages of a book, or by following the explicit directions of a tourist brochure—you have to get out there, to walk, talk, breathe, explore and live it for yourself. The limited aim of this small book is to make the experience of *living* in Dublin a little easier.

I make no apologies for the criticisms of institutions or facilities mentioned in the book; hopefully, if there are subsequent editions of the book, such criticisms will no longer be necessary. Every effort has been made to provide accurate information; I apologise for omissions or factual errors, and again hope that in future editions, with the advantage of outside criticism, advice and suggestions, the many shortcomings will be eliminated.

My sincere thanks to Matt McNulty, Manager of Dublin Tourism, for his kind assistance; to Bernard Share and Maurice Craig for their contributions; to Paula Anderson and Siun Kearney for typing the manuscript; to Anna Boylan of Gill and Macmillan, now Mrs Tony Farmar of Macmillan for encouragement, and to Mary Dowey of Gill and Macmillan for her patience and invaluable help throughout.

DUBLIN

A Personal View. *Maurice Craig*

THE editor and I met to discuss my contribution to this book in a particularly pleasant pub off Grafton Street. Not long before we left we overheard the manager telling somebody that the pub was to be closed that evening, it had been bought for £200,000 or some such unreal sum and was going to be turned into a hotel or an office-block or some such unreal kind of building.

After a certain age almost any change seems to be a change for the worse, at least until it has happened. I was at school in Dublin from 1926 till 1933, but I remember almost nothing about the central city except that the Four Courts was being rebuilt and that there were tram-standards down the middle of Pembroke Road and Baggot Street, and what seemed vast areas of space around Leeson Street Bridge. Later on I came to know central Dublin very well indeed; but even then hardly anything had changed. The bookshops on the quays were full of eighteenth-century books, there were still steamboats plying between Kingsbridge and the Custom House, and the tottering tenements of Dominick Street and Gardiner Street and York Street were still outwardly intact. Harry Clarke's Beardsleyesque frontispiece to the 1913–21 Abercrombie Dublin Plan, a sheeted white-faced ghost brooding over a half-ruined city under a jet-black sky, entitled 'The Last Hour of the Night', still seemed relevant. The Abercrombie Plan itself was a visionary document of baleful import, for the most part, but we still lived in the Dublin of Louis MacNeice

> . . . the air soft on the cheek
> And porter running from the taps
> With a head of yellow cream
> And Nelson on his pillar
> Watching his world collapse.

'Historic with guns and vermin' he called her: odd words for a lover, yet they were written in love. It was Dublin of barrel-organs by the balustrades, of the old harp-player in Duke Street, of the barefooted newsboys crying 'Hegglamail'. And, as I said before, of dusty bookshelves laden with eighteenth-century calf and even the odd bit of morocco. But now we are too rich to drink porter, and even 'a pint' is not inevitably a pint of stout. We are not magnanimous enough to have left Nelson, or even his Pillar, standing where they were. We are not nearly rich enough, however, to have any eighteenth-century calf, except in cosseted captivity. We have cleaned up most of our best buildings and pulled down a few of our second-best.

But Dublin is still the strumpet city of Denis Johnston's play and James Plunkett's novel, suckling her bastard brood. We have invented Irish Coffee, or, to be exact, we have given a name to what we always used to do whenever we had the money. We have stopped distilling whiskey in Dublin. The last passenger-ship has left the North Wall. Some of us are afraid to swim at Sandycove or Sandymount or Clontarf. Our universities are bursting at the seams, and one of them has migrated to the suburbs.

I hardly ever meet anyone who lives in Dublin and would rather live somewhere else. A few people who spent a middle-class childhood here complain that it is too small: I know very well what they mean, and am thankful to have been born in Belfast. Rather more people complain that it is too big, and I know what they mean, too. If the centre of Dublin was the right size in 1800 or 1900 or even 1950, it must be too small now, when featureless

14

suburbs have eaten into so much of the surrounding country.

Of course Dublin *is* beautiful. To begin with, it is so beautiful on the map: the wide encircling arms of the bay, the smaller circle of the canals and the circular roads, the not quite straight river running through the middle, the Liffey valley above Chapelizod leading to the pastures of Kildare, the mountains at a civilised distance to the south. There is the quality of light, especially on an autumn evening from a high window in one of the squares; the continental quality of the out-door life in O'Connell Street, long after dark; the colour of the brickwork in the centre, and the ubiquity of random walling of Dublin calp or Dalkey granite in the older suburbs and all along the coast to Killiney and beyond. Even without the architectural set-pieces in all their splendour—the two great riverside masterpieces, the Bank and Trinity, the King's Inns and the Blue-Coat School hidden where only the curious can find them, the Royal Hospital where more than curiosity is needed to get a decent view of it—even without these Dublin has a wide variety of comely houses, from the great four-storey mansions of the squares and the streets adjoining them, to the majestic Pembroke Road with its massive flights of steps, the raised basements of Ballsbridge and Rathgar, the paired venetian-gothic doorways and wide Victorian eaves, tiny houses entered by a flight of steps to their upper floors, seaside boxes with their lions and eagles among the granite outcrops of the coast. And every so often there is a Martello tower constructed with the precision and solidity of a lighthouse.

And what splendid views there are from the upper rooms of Dublin houses, down their long garden vistas, granite walls topped with valerian where the cats sun themselves, and the coach-house at the end with its little round windows. And if from one side of the house the distant view is dominated by the Great Gasometer or the barber's-pole chimney at the Pigeon House, from the other side you can probably see the mountains. And as you go out, you can ponder yet again the purpose of that mysterious brass rail curving out at breast-height in the hall, which the uncharitable ascribe to the drinking habits of our forebears, and with luck you can admire one of those massive mahogany-cased Irish locks with its brass mountings.

It used to be a two-edged compliment frequently paid to Dublin that it was easy to get out of, to the mountains or the country or the sea. It is not an attitude towards towns which I want to encourage; yet I can see that it is both more desirable, and less easy, to get out of Dublin than it used to be. Downtown Dublin is not dead, nor even dying, but it is no longer in the best of health. All my favourite restaurants of a quarter of a century ago are either closed or changed out of all recognition. Eating out was never Dublin's strongest point (by comparison with other capitals or university towns), but it now seems to me to have lost all its savour. Perhaps this is nothing but middle-aged dyspepsia, since I drink in central Dublin with greater pleasure and with more discrimination (and less frequently) than I used to do.

Dublin pubs are not what they used to be, yet a surprising number have survived the onset of affluence. Only a few days ago I noticed to my delighted surprise that an old-fashioned pub in a very central situation which had for many months been boarded-up, to all appearances ready for the chopper, was open again and has escaped 'improvement'. And, to be fair, there are a few among the brand-new pubs which are fit to drink in.

The Dublin that matters to me is a city of quays and wharves and ships, of quays and bridges and bookshops, of pubs and churches and libraries. Dublin may not be big enough to have an opera-house (at least until we very drastically revise our priorities), and in this respect to have to live without escape, in Dublin would be a privation. But in the matter of libraries what riches! what variety! Trinity Old and Trinity New, Marsh's, the National more full of ghosts than any, though so much younger, the King's Inn, the Royal Irish Academy, the Gilbert in Pearse Street, the

Antiquaries in Merrion Square, the Worth in Steevens' Hospital. All with their different and inimitable atmospheres. Newest and most remarkable of all is the marvellous Chester Beatty in Shrewsbury Road while further out there are the monastic libraries such as Milltown and Killiney and, of course, Maynooth.

There has been a mortality among the churches: they tend to suffer from the same disease as pubs: dusty empty ones in the centre of town, large ugly crowded ones on the periphery. But the Pro-Cathedral and St Andrew's, Westland Row, have been cleaned up, and St Catherine's saved from the fury of the Finaghy Methodists to live again in the revival of the Liberties. A similar effort is saving the Tailors' Hall.

There is one aspect of Dublin's size which I must admit to finding most agreeable. It means that a comparatively unimportant person such as myself is usually an acquaintance, and sometimes also a friend, of a good many of those who run the major institutions of the country. As Claud Cockburn has observed in his autobiography, this is a function of the small size of Ireland, not just that of Dublin, and it is not so much a matter of social or intellectual snobbery—or managerial snobbery if there is such a thing?—as of that current vogue-word, participation. Claud Cockburn, I need hardly say, would know everyone who mattered, wherever he might live.

There may be an Establishment in Dublin: I am not very sensitive about such things so I cannot be sure. Certainly there are a few key names which crop up over and over again in conversations as being people who are on the inside and can get things done. Some of them I have met: most of them I have not. Dublin has its share of people who are famous for being famous: it always had, in my opinion, and only charity towards the dead prevents me from mentioning some names, from the supposedly golden past. If there is indeed an Establishment in Dublin, it is certainly not well-defined at the edges, and we still rub shoulders, as we always did, with people whom in another city we would probably never meet.

Can this flavour, these impalpable social filaments, survive the strains of the growth which, we are promised, will continue to be thrust upon us? Urbanism, and its cousin urbanity, is a delicate amalgam of architecture, social habit, economics and transport. Every two or three years we are presented with a massive study of some aspect of Dublin's development, usually from some prestigious overseas consultant. Underground railways, which have not been heard of since the visionary days of Abercrombie, have surfaced again—if that is the right way of putting it. Nobody wants Dublin to stagnate or die in the middle, and a vigorous section of the younger generation seems determined to save her. More power to them. More Power to them too, even if from now on it must be distilled in Cork.

PLACES OF INTEREST

CATHEDRALS AND CHURCHES

Christ Church Cathedral, Lord Edward Street, Dublin 2

Founded in 1038 by King Sitric and Donatus, Bishop of Dublin. Demolished by the Normans in 1172, and rebuilt by them during the next fifty years. One of the main points of interest is the tomb of Strongbow. While King James II was in Dublin in 1689, the Cathedral was seized, and for a brief period the rites of the pre-Reformation faith were restored and mass celebrated in the King's presence. Christ Church is the traditional venue for Dubliners welcoming in the New Year : songs, drink and tolerant policemen, but it's not quite Piccadilly Circus.

Visiting hours : 0930 to 1730 May to September and 0930 to 1600 October to April

Buses : 21, 21A, 78, 78A, 78B

St Patrick's Cathedral, Patrick Street, Dublin 2

Close to Christ Church, and also Church of Ireland,

St Patrick's was founded in 1190 by John Comyn, first Anglo-Norman Archbishop of Dublin. The architecture is described as 'early English', the square tower being added in the fourteenth century, and the two-hundred foot spire in the eighteenth century. It is mainly associated with Jonathan Swift, who was Dean of the Cathedral from 1713 to 1745, and whose tomb is there. There are also monuments to John Philpot Curran the orator, Samuel Lover, novelist and poet and Turlough O'Carolan, the great Irish harpist. In the fourteenth century the Cathedral housed a university, later suppressed by Henry VIII. The Cathedral was extensively restored in the mid-nineteenth century by a member of the Guinness family.

Visiting hours : 0830 to 1800 each day
Buses : 50, 50A, 50B, 54, 54A, 54B

St Michan's Church, Church Street, Dublin 7

Dating from the seventeenth century, though erected on the site of a Danish church founded in 1096. The square tower is believed to date from the Danish period. The vaults are world-renowned; bodies, including one of an eight-foot tall crusader have lain there for centuries showing no signs of decomposition.

Visiting hours : Monday to Friday 1000 to 1245; 1400 to 1645
Saturday 1000 to 1245
Buses : 34, 34A, 38A
Vaults : Admission 10p and children 5p; closed on Sundays

St Mary's Church, Mary Street, Dublin 1

Built in 1627; Theobald Wolfe Tone, founder of the United Irishmen, was baptised there, and his death mask is on view. Playwright Seán O'Casey was also baptised in the Church.

Visiting hours : Monday to Friday 1400 to 1700 May to September
Buses : all those going to the city centre, from which the church is 10 minutes' walk

St Audoen's Church, High Street, Dublin 8

Founded by the Normans in the late twelfth century, and dedicated to St Ouen of Rouen, it is the oldest of the city's parish churches, and though partially ruined, it is still used for public worship. The tower dates from the twelfth century, and three of the six bells were cast in the early fifteenth century, making them the oldest in Ireland.
Open : Sundays only, 1015 to 1115 for Morning Service. Other visits by appointment
Buses : 21, 21A, 78, 78A, 78B

St Werburgh's Church, Werburgh Street (off Christchurch Place), Dublin 8

Originally erected towards the end of the twelfth century, the present church dates from 1718, and thanks to recent restoration is perhaps the most perfect Georgian church in Dublin. There are twenty-seven vaults beneath the church, one containing the remains of Lord Edward Fitzgerald. Admission is free. Apply to the sexton, 8 Castle Street, around the corner from the church.
Visiting hours : 1000 to 1600 on weekdays
Buses : 21, 21A, 50, 50A, 50B, 54, 78, 78A, 78B

Pro-Cathedral, Marlboro Street, Dublin 1

Built in the early nineteenth century, in Grecian-Doric style, the portico is copied from the Theseum in Athens, and the interior is modelled on the Church of St Philippe du Roule in Paris. It is situated parallel to O'Connell Street, Dublin 1. For Services *see* **Church Services.**
Open : 0700 to 2130 each day
Buses : all those going to or through the city centre

BUILDINGS

The Custom House, Dublin 1

On the north bank of the river Liffey, beside Butt Bridge, designed by the English architect, James Gandon, it was completed in 1791. It is undoubtedly one of Dublin's finest buildings; quadrangular in shape, the pavilions at either end are decorated with the arms of Ireland. There is a central dome rising 125 feet surmounted by a statue of Hope. Destroyed in 1921 during the War of Independence, the building has been faithfully restored.

Buses : all those passing over O'Connell Bridge from which it is 5 minutes' walk

Bank of Ireland, College Green, Dublin 2

Formerly the Irish Houses of Parliament, where the Act of Union was passed in 1800. Begun in 1729, it was the first of the great eighteenth-century buildings to be erected in Dublin. The original design is by Sir Edward Lovat Pierce, but the east front is by James Gandon. The most striking architectural feature is the complete absence of frontal windows. It is open during normal banking hours (1000 to 1230 and 1330 to 1500 Monday to Friday) and any of the liveried attendants will show visitors around, free of charge.

Buses : all those going through College Street or Westmoreland Street

The Four Courts, Inns Quay, Dublin 7

Originally designed by Thomas Cooley, the plans were modified and completed by James Gandon. There is a 450-foot frontage, supported by a portico of six Corinthian columns, and statues of Moses, flanked by Justice and Mercy. The entrance hall is surmounted by a vast dome, 64 feet in diameter. The building houses the Supreme and High Courts, and court sittings are open to the public. It is 15 minutes' walk from O'Connell Bridge.

Buses : 23, 24, 25, 34, 38, 39, 39A, 51, 72, 79

The General Post Office, O'Connell Street, Dublin 1

Used as the headquarters of the Irish Volunteers during the 1916 rebellion, the G.P.O. remains a symbol of the Republican spirit, and is used as the rallying point for public demonstrations and protests almost every weekend. Built in 1818, it was shelled by a British gunboat in 1916, and severely damaged by fire. It has since been restored and is now used (as the name suggests) as the central post office. For services *see* **Post Offices.**

Buses : all those going to or through city centre

Dublin Castle, Dame Street, Dublin 2

Built in the early thirteenth century, on the site of a ninth-century Danish fortress, Dublin Castle was the centre of English rule in Ireland for almost eight hundred years. The Record Tower, in the lower Castle Yard, dates from 1205, and the Bermingham Tower, the tallest in the Castle, dates from the early fifteenth century. It was from here that the Northern Chieftains Red Hugh O'Donnell, Henry and Art O'Neill, escaped on Christmas Eve 1591. The Gothic-styled Church of the Holy Trinity is more recent in origin; designed by Francis Johnston it was built in 1807. The State Apartments where the first President of Ireland, Dr Douglas Hyde, was inaugurated in 1938, are open from Monday to Friday, 1000 to 1215; 1400 to 1700. Admission 10p, and 5p for children. Dublin Castle also houses the Garda headquarters, and Special Branch, and the Castle Yard is always open.

Buses : 21, 21A, 50, 50A, 50B, 54, 54A, 56

The City Hall, Lord Edward Street, Dublin 2

Erected between 1769 and 1779, City Hall is beside Dublin Castle and was designed by Thomas Cooley. Originally the Royal Exchange, it was taken over by Dublin Corporation in 1852, and since that time it has been the headquarters of the municipal administration. The mace and sword of the city, 102 Royal Charters, and the assembly Rolls of the Corporation are all housed here; everything in fact except the Dublin City Council which was abolished by the government in 1969 and which shows no sign of being revived.

Open : 0915 to 1245 and 1415 to 1645

Buses : 21, 21A, 50, 50A, 50B, 54, 54A, 56

The Mansion House, Dawson Street, Dublin 2

A very attractive Queen Anne style building which has been the official residence of the Lord Mayor of Dublin since 1715. Daniel O'Connell is among the people to have held office as Lord Mayor. The first Dáil met here from January to September 1919, and the adoption of the Declaration of Independence in 1919 and the signing of the Truce which ended Anglo-Irish hostilities in July 1921 both took place here.

Open : 1000 to 2100

Buses : 4, 10, 11, 11A, 11B, 13, 14, 14A, 15A, 15B, 20, 46A, 64A, 86

Trinity College, College Green, Dublin 2

Founded by Queen Elizabeth I in 1591 on the site of the Priory of All Hallowes, which was suppressed by Henry VIII. The site of the Priory's High Altar is marked by the Campanile in the front square, a bell-tower built by the Protestant Primate, John George Beresford in 1852. The tower is one hundred feet tall, and the bell weighs almost two tons. The University was expressly intended to further the Reformation in Ireland, and until just two years ago, Irish Catholics wishing to attend Trinity were supposed to obtain the permission of their bishop. The buildings date from the eighteenth and nineteenth century, and are attractively laid out in cobblestone courtyards. At the entrance to the Front Gate, there are statues by John Foley of orator Edmund Burke and playwright Oliver Goldsmith, both former students of the College. Past the Campanile on the right is the Old Library (*see* **Libraries**) where the Book of Kells is on display.

Visiting hours : Monday to Friday 1000 to 1700

Saturday 1000 to 1300

Buses : all those going through College Street and Westmoreland Street

Kilmainham Jail, Kilmainham, Dublin 8

Erected in 1796, a number of Irish patriots were imprisoned or executed there. It was closed in 1924, but

since 1966, due to voluntary work by preservationists it has been restored as a museum and is open to visitors from 1500 to 1700 Sundays only. Admission 5p, children 3p.
Buses : 21, 23, 24, 78, 78A, 79
Telephone : 755990.

Leinster House, Kildare Street, Dublin 2

Designed by Richard Cassells, it was built in 1745 as the residence of the Duke of Leinster, James Fitzgerald, on the then unfashionable south side of the city. At the time Fitzgerald declared, 'Where I go fashion will follow', and time has proved him right. Acquired by the Royal Dublin Society in 1815. From 1922 it has housed the Irish parliament, which consists of a Lower House (Dáil) and Upper House (Seanad). Visitors may attend debates in the public gallery. Application for tickets should be made to a member of the Dáil or Seanad, to the appropriate Embassy or to the Superintendent's Office at the Kildare Street entrance. Attendance of members is very poor, and the quality of debate is for the most part undistinguished.
Buses : as for the Mansion House from which it is
5 minutes' walk.
Telephone : 60441

GEORGIAN DUBLIN

This, the most characteristic aspect of Dublin architecture, is vanishing fast, thanks to the voracious appetite of the property developers. The stately Merrion Square is still intact, as is Fitzwilliam Square, but Mountjoy Square fights a losing battle and St Stephen's Green and Hume Street have clearly been lost. The Irish Georgian Society and An Taisce (The National Trust) protect what they can; witness the magnificent restoration of the Tailors Hall. The finest interiors can be seen in what is now the Bank of Ireland, College Green, and the ceiling of the Rotunda Hospital Chapel, Parnell Square, is magnificent

24

There is a good ceiling too in Ely Hall, Ely Place. For further details contact : **Irish Georgian Society,** 50 Mountjoy Square, tel. 41494. Architectural Library facilities available by appointment. Also **An Taisce,** The National Trust, Bridge House, Dublin 4, tel. 64023.

The Botanic Gardens, Botanic Road, Glasnevin, Dublin 9
   Originally the land surrounded the house of essayist Thomas Addison; later the Royal Dublin Society bought the estate from poet Thomas Tickell, and in 1795 the National Botanic Gardens were founded 'to increase and foster taste for practical and scientific botany'. Since 1901 the Gardens have been administered by the Department of Agriculture. The 50 acres comprise a wide range of flowers, trees, shrubs and tropical plants. Admission is free and the Gardens are open on weekdays, 0900 to 1800 in summer, 1000 to 1630 in winter, and on Sundays 1100 to 1800 in summer and 1100 to 1630 in winter. On Sundays the greenhouses do not open until 1400.
Buses : 13, 19, 34, 34A
Telephone : 374388

Phœnix Park/Zoological Gardens : *see* **Young People in Dublin**

Dunsink Observatory : Castleknock, Co. Dublin
   One of the oldest observatories in the world, Dunsink was founded in 1783. It is north of Phœnix Park, between Finglas and Blanchardstown, and is open to the public on the first Saturday of each month, from September to April, between 2000 and 2200.
Bus : 40 from Lower Abbey Street
Telephone : 383887

Bull Island :
   This bird sanctuary is truly unique : nowhere else in the world can Brent Geese which travel from the Arctic Circle be seen so easily within the boundaries of a capital

city. Among the other species to be seen are wigeon, teal, shoveler, pintail, goldeneye, oystercatcher and dunlin.

Buses : 30 from Marlboro Street to the Bull Wall from where it is 5 minutes' walk

For **places of interest** *see* **Map of Central Dublin** pp. 45-48.

DAY TRIPS FROM DUBLIN

Avoca, Co. Wicklow

Where the river Avonmore meets the river Avonbeg, immortalised in Thomas Moore's 'The Meeting of the Waters'. There is even a tree where the poet, enchanted, stood composing.

Blessington, Co. Wicklow

A picturesque and as yet unspoiled village on the north side of Blessington Reservoir which was created by the Poulaphouca hydro-electric station on the river Liffey. There are a number of natural and artificial lakes in the area, such as Lough Dan, Lough Tay and Roundwood Reservoir. Pleasant for picnicking. Can be reached by the 65 bus.

Glendalough, Co. Wicklow

Associated with St Kevin; the remains of his sixth-century monastic settlement, including St Kevin's Church and the Round Tower are situated beside the Lower Lake. C.I.E. operate day tours in the summer but Glendalough may also be reached by one of the few remaining privately-run bus companies, St Kevin's Bus Service, which leaves St Stephen's Green West (opposite the College of Surgeons) twice a day in the summer, at 1130 and 1815, in winter the bus runs at 1815 each evening and at 1115 as well on Friday, Saturday and Sunday only. The bus also stops at Bray, Calgary, Roundwood, Annamoe and Laragh.

Greystones, Co. Wicklow

On the east coast, Greystones is a popular but quiet, rather English seaside resort. There are tennis courts, good swimming both from rocks and sandy beaches, and it is reached by the 84 bus, from College Street (beside Trinity College).

Bray, Co. Wicklow

Very English—a popular commercialised seaside town, a mini-Blackpool in fact, with little to recommend it, except its commercialism. The 'dodgem cars' on the seafront are very good.

Enniskerry, Co. Wicklow

13 miles from Dublin, Enniskerry is a delightful, unspoilt village. Close by is the entrance to Powerscourt Estate. The beautifully designed Japanese and Italian gardens are open to the public from Easter to October 1030 to 1730. Admission is 25p for adults, 15p for children. There are also a deerpark and a 300-foot waterfall open to the public throughout the year. It is reached by the 44 bus from Poolbeg Street, Dublin 2.

Rathfarnham

4 miles from the city, Rathfarnham is situated at the foot of the Dublin mountains. Rathfarnham Castle, now owned by the Jesuit Order, has its own meteorological office and seismograph. About one mile from the village is St Enda's, the Irish-speaking school founded by Padraic Pearse, one of the leaders of the rebellion of 1916. From Rathfarnham you can reach the Pine Forest, and the tiny village of Glencree, which has a youth hostel. On Mount Pelier Hill, there are the remains of the infamous Hell Fire Club, whose members indulged in some spectacular orgies in the eighteenth century.

Castletown House

12 miles from Dublin, at Celbridge village in Co. Kildare, Castletown is one of the finest of Ireland's stately

homes. It was built in 1722 for William Connolly, Speaker of the Irish House of Commons, and designed by Alessandro Galilei, the architect of St John Lateran, in Rome. It is now the headquarters of the Irish Georgian Society, and is open to the public from 1 April to 31 September, on Wednesdays, Saturdays and Sundays from 1400 to 1800. Admission is 25p for adults, 5p for children. During the summer there are regular Sunday night concerts and plays with special transport arranged, and in June, Castletown and nearby Carton House provide a magnificent setting for the concerts and recitals of the Festival of Great Irish Houses. The 67 bus from Bachelor's Walk will leave you at the gate.

Carton House

14 miles from Dublin and 1 mile from Maynooth, Carton House was built between 1739 and 1747 for the Duke of Leinster. One of the most recent occupants was film actor Peter Sellers. Among the features of the house are the Gold Saloon with its magnificent organ and the Chinese Room, decorated around 1752. Open to the public on Saturdays, Sundays and bank holidays, 1400 to 1800 from Easter to the end of September. Admission is 30p for adults, 10p for children. The 66 bus from Bachelor's Walk passes the entrance to the estate.

Howth

9 miles north-east of the city, Howth is a picturesque fishing port, with a good harbour, and swimming facilities at Claremont and Balscadden Bay. You can buy fresh fish from the shops on the quays at a fraction of the price it would cost in most Dublin shops. About half a mile from the village is Howth Castle and Gardens, built in the mid-fourteenth century and home of the St Lawrence family, who have been associated with the Howth area since the twelfth century. The Castle is not open to the public, but the magnificent gardens with the famous Beech Hedge Walk—thirty feet in height and half a mile in length—and

the superb collection of rhododendrons are open to the public each day from 1100 to 1800 from Easter to mid-September, and to 2100 during May and June. Admission is 5p for adults, 2½p for children, and the estate can be reached by the 31 bus from Lower Abbey Street.

Newgrange, Co. Meath

There are prehistoric burial chambers or tumuli at Newgrange, Knowth and Dowth, near Slane, dating from the Bronze Age. Newgrange which dates from 2000 B.C. is the most important of European passage graves, consisting of a huge cairn of loose stones, 44 feet in height, covered with soil, trees and bushes. Twelve stones encircle the tomb—there were originally 35 and a 60-foot passage leads to the 20-foot-high tomb chamber itself, from which there are 3 elaborately decorated recesses. New Grange is open to the public every day except Monday, from 1000 to 1800 and a guide is available. Admission is 10p for adults, 5p for children. Tours are arranged by C.I.E. through the Boyne valley throughout the summer, tel. 46301.

COACH TOURS

C.I.E. operate a number of coach tours from 1 May to 1 September. The most comprehensive (and expensive) is the **Minstrel Tour of Dublin's Fair City,** which leaves Busaras at 1500 each weekday, and visits the places and buildings associated with Synge, Joyce, Shaw, Swift and O'Casey. Dinner and a 3-hour cabaret end the day, and the cost is about £3.50 per person. A shorter tour from 1500 to 1900, which does not include dinner or cabaret costs £1.15 per person (children under 15 are charged 60p). There are also coach tours to **Glendalough, Powerscourt,** the **Liffey valley,** the **Boyne valley, Wexford** and **Athlone.** There are combined coach tours and cruises to **Lough Derg** on the river Shannon, and day tours to the **Slieve Bloom mountains** and **Roscrea.** Similar tours depart from

Dún Laoghaire railway station, from the end of May. Details of tours, times and costs are available from C.I.E. tours department, 35 Lower Abbey Street, Dublin 1, tel. 300777.

RAIL TOURS

This will be the twenty-third year of C.I.E.'s very popular 'radio' train tours. Musical programmes are interspersed with commentaries on places of interest. The all-in fare includes train reservation, lunch and high tea on the train, a tour by jaunting car in Killarney or by bus in Connemara. The **Killarney** tour leaves Amiens Street Station at 0935 and returns at 2215, costing £5.00 for adults and £3.40 for children under 15. The **Connemara** tour leaves Amiens Street Station at 0945 and returns at 2105, costing £4.50 for adults and £3.20 for children. There are also combined train and coach tours to the **Mountains of Mourne, Armagh** and **Carlingford Peninsula,** costing on average £1.70 for adults, and 85p for children. Details and booking at C.I.E. tours, 35 Lower Abbey Street, Dublin 1, tel. 300777.

CULTURE AND ENTERTAINMENT

THEATRE

IF there ever was an Irish theatrical tradition, a rather doubtful claim, it is not much in evidence in Ireland today. Our reputation for theatre rests with our playwrights (mostly dead) and our actors (mostly exported). Except for a few brief periods, such as the Abbey seasons in the 'twenties and the Mac Liammóir/Edwards company in the 'thirties and 'forties, Dublin has lacked a consistent theatrical movement, and certainly theatre in the city today is at a particularly low ebb.

There is only one full-time repertory company, which occupies two theatres, the **Abbey** and the **Peacock**. The two largest theatres, the **Olympia** and the **Gaiety**, correspond to English provincial variety theatres, presenting ballet, concerts, opera, pantomime and straight plays. As yet, however, they haven't resorted to all-in wrestling. There are five other theatres, the part-time Irish-language **Damer Hall**, the **Gate** which receives a government subsidy, the **Eblana**, and two very small theatres, the **Focus** and the **Lantern**, which between them seat less than 250 people. Experimental theatre is normally left to the two university theatre groups and both have performances open to the public; **Trinity College** at **Players Theatre**, 4 Trinity College, and **University College** at the **Aula Maxima**, 86 St Stephen's Green. The **Project Arts Centre** in Abbey Street also occasionally presents experimental plays, usually at lunchtime. The annual Dublin Theatre Festival which runs for a fortnight each March presents about a dozen Irish and world premieres.

It is advisable to book in advance for the theatre, particularly for Friday and Saturday nights. Booking can usually be done at the theatre itself, at the **Central Booking Agency**, 29 Lower O'Connell Street (tel. 42769) or at **Brown Thomas** (tel. 776861) or **Switzer's** (tel. 776821) in Grafton Street. Telephone booking is permitted but in this case tickets must usually be collected at least an hour before the curtain rises. Prices are relatively cheap, certainly less expensive than New York or London. The curtain is always advertised to rise at 2000 but seldom does. Dress is always informal. Theatres advertise their plays in the *Irish Times, Irish Press, Irish Independent, Evening Press* and *Evening Herald*. One more thing: theatre programmes are in most cases overpriced advertisement sheets, costing 10p.

Abbey: Lower Abbey Street, Dublin 1. Tel. 44505

Home of the National Theatre Company, which counts among its past directors W. B. Yeats, Lady Gregory and J. M. Synge. The present directors are less distinguished, as, often, are the accomplishments of the theatre. There is a steady diet of plays by Yeats, Lady Gregory, Synge, Brendan Behan and Seán O'Casey, mixed with what are often rather mediocre contemporary plays. It is advisable to book well in advance for the summer months, as the tourist-orientated repertoire is inexplicably popular with foreign visitors. The bar serves alcohol and coffee, and drinks for the interval can be ordered before the show. Two other good points, a free cast list is provided as an alternative to the programme, which in the Abbey's case is good value anyway, and the ladies in the box-office are particularly friendly and helpful.

Prices : 30p, 45p, 60p, 75p and £1.00, with special rates for students

Peacock : Lower Abbey Street, Dublin 1. Tel. 44505 or, after 1900, 48738

Intended as the Abbey's experimental theatre, it sometimes does experiment but suffers from its close links with the parent company. However the Peacock presentations are generally more interesting and better produced than those of the Abbey, due largely to the talent and commitment of the younger members of the company. During the year there is a programme of lunchtime events, plays, poetry-readings, concerts, etc., a children's theatre club on Saturday afternoons, and a schools' programme which introduces and propagates the use of drama in education.

Prices : 30p, 50p and 75p

Gaiety : South King Street, Dublin 2. Tel. 771717

Built in 1871 it has since been modernised but retains much of its original elegance. The theatre is used by the Dublin Grand Opera Society for their spring and autumn seasons (*see* **Opera**), by the R.T.E. Symphony Orchestra for Sunday night concerts (*see* **Music**), and for pantomime at Christmas, variety in the summer, and in between an occasional straight play. There are bars on all floors.

Prices : Variable, usually 40p to £1.00

Olympia : 72 Dame Street, Dublin 2. Tel. 778962

The largest theatre in Dublin, the Olympia presents similar *divertissements* to those at the Gaiety. The 'gods' (uppermost balcony) provide the cheapest seats in town—well, not quite seats, you have to sit on wooden steps, but they do say that's the real way to see theatre. There are bars on all floors.

Prices : 20p to £1.00

Eblana : Busaras, Store Street, Dublin 1. Tel. 46707

Located in the central bus station, the Eblana is a small intimate theatre leased by Amalgamated Artists, who mix international hits with an occasional home-grown product. Despite a tendency to go for the risqué (which isn't) the theatre fulfils a need in presenting a large number of plays which Dubliners would otherwise never see. There is a bar upstairs in the main building.

Prices : 35p to 50p

Gate : Cavendish Row, Dublin 1. Tel. 43722

Home of the Mac Liammóir/Edwards Theatre company, who since 1928 have together presented over 350 productions. The theatre closed recently for renovations, but reopened in March 1971, with a government subsidy enabling Michael Mac Liammóir and Hilton Edwards to present plays for six months each year, and make the theatre available to other companies for the remaining six months. Coffee is served; the nearest bar is directly across the road in Groome's Hotel.

Prices : 40p to 75p

Focus : off Pembroke Street, Dublin 2.

A tiny theatre attached to Ireland's only Stanislavsky Studio, run by Deirdre O'Connell, ex-Actors' Studio, New York. As the 75-seat theatre is not self-supporting, the actors must hold down other jobs, with the result that no more than four or five plays are produced annually, mainly American and Continental classics. 'Improvisational eve-

B

nings' are arranged, usually on Sundays. Coffee is served. Booking is through Brown Thomas and Disc Finder, 147 Lower Baggot Street, tel. 60429.
Prices : 35p and 45p

Lantern : 38 Merrion Square, Dublin 2. Tel. 61741 (after 1900)

The smallest of Dublin's theatres, the Lantern presents about a dozen plays a year, from a very wide repertoire. Booking is through Brown Thomas, and tickets can be collected after 1900, but at least 15 minutes before the show begins.
Prices : 35p and 45p

For Theatres in central Dublin *see* **Map pp. 36-39.**

CINEMA

DUBLIN is reputed to have the highest cinema-going population of any capital city in western Europe. Certainly the existence of a thriving black market in movie tickets, and the fact that in the past 6 years 8 cinemas have been added to the already large list, would support this reputation. The popularity of cinema in Dublin is contrary to international trends and all the more surprising in view of the fact that too many film theatres are uncomfortable, old-fashioned and in some cases just plain dirty, while all films shown are subjected to annoyingly erratic government censorship. Prices, however, are much lower than in other capital cities, ranging usually from 30p to £1.00 (less in the suburbs). Certain cinemas offer reduced rates for old-age pensioners for afternoon shows. Sundays are by far the most popular nights, and it is necessary to book in advance or you will risk paying up to 100 per cent more on the black market which operates in O'Connell Street. Saturday comes next in popularity and then Wednesday nights. Details of programmes and times are listed in the *Irish Times* and both evening newspapers. Many of the cinemas have late-night films at the weekend.

One other thing: we slavishly follow the British tradition of playing our National Anthem at every possible opportunity, at the cinema, theatre, dog-shows, etc., and we expect everyone to stand rigidly to attention while it is being played. The original practice involved facing the national flag, and in a quaint case of Pavlovian conditioning, every day at cinemas, theatres and dog-shows throughout the country, thousands of otherwise quite sensible people stand facing where a flag should be but seldom is displayed. Only the most athletic can escape this rather pointless exercise.

Academy : Pearse Street, Dublin 2. Late night films as an extra attraction Saturday and Sunday. Tel. 774994

Adelphi, 1, 2, 3 : Middle Abbey Street, Dublin 1. Tel. 42667

Ambassador : Parnell Square, Dublin 1. Tel. 44460

Astor : Eden Quay, Dublin 1. Late show Saturday. Tel. 48641

Capitol : 45 Talbot Street, Dublin 1. Tel. 43639

Carlton : Upper O'Connell Street, Dublin 1. Late show Friday and Saturday. Tel. 44098

Corinthian : Eden Quay, Dublin 1. Late show Saturday. Tel. 44611

Curzon : Middle Abbey Street, Dublbin 1. Late show Saturday and Sunday. Tel. 47469

Film Centre : O'Connell Bridge House, Dublin 2. Late show Friday and Saturday. Tel. 778923

Grafton : Grafton Street, Dublin 2. Late show Saturday and Sunday. Tel. 773206

Green : St Stephen's Green, Dublin 2. Late show Friday and Saturday. Tel. 751573

International : Earlsfort Terrace, Dublin 2. Tel. 64207

New Metropole : Townsend Street, Dublin 2.

Plaza : Cinerama, Parnell Square, Dublin 1. Late show Friday and Saturday. Tel. 46146

Regent : Findlater's Place, Dublin 1. Tel. 48145

Savoy, 1, 2 : Upper O'Connell Street, Dublin 1. Tel. 48487

For cinemas in central Dublin *see* **Map** on following pages.

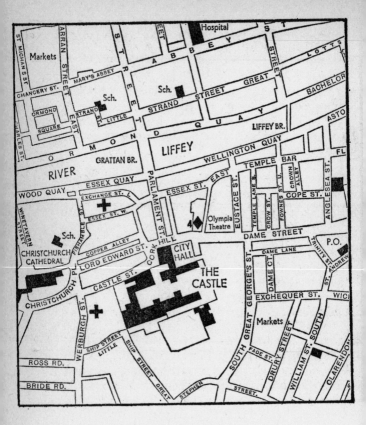

Theatres

4. Olympia

Map of Central Dublin showing Theatres and Cinemas

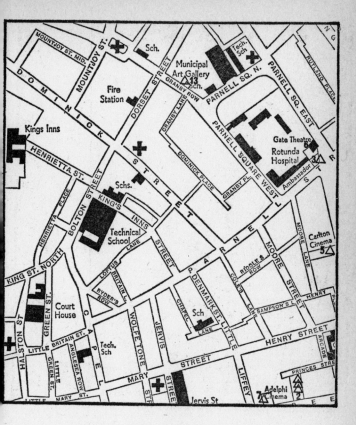

 Theatres

6. Gate

△ **Cinemas**

2. Adelphi 1, 2, 3   7. Curzon
3. Ambassador   13. Plaza
5. Carlton

Map of Central Dublin showing Theatres and Cinemas

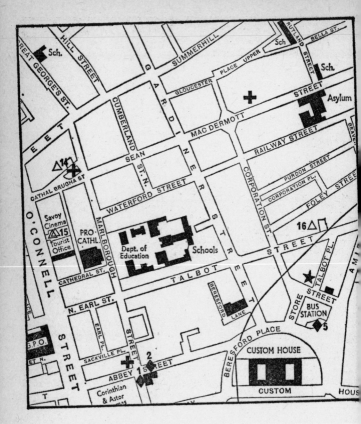

	Theatres		△ Cinemas
1. Abbey		14. Regent	
2. Peacock		15. Savoy	
5. Eblana		16. Capitol	

Map of Central Dublin showing Theatres and Cinemas

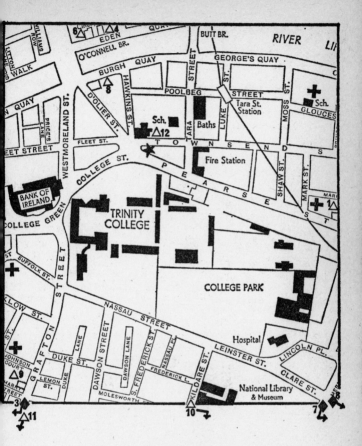

♦ **Theatres**

3. Gaiety
7. Focus
8. Lantern

△ **Cinemas**

1. Academy
4. Astor
6. Corinthian
8. Film Centre
9. Grafton
10. International
11. Green
12. Metropole

Map of Central Dublin showing Theatres and Cinemas

National Gallery of Ireland, Merrion Square, Dublin 2.
Tel. 67571; after hours tel. 61699

Opened in 1864 and originally based on the collection of
William Dargan, one of the organisers of the Great Exhibi-
tion of 1853, the gallery has, through various bequests,
including those of Sir Hugh Lane, Edward Martyn, Sir
Alfred Chester Beatty and George Bernard Shaw, built up
an extensive collection of paintings from all the European
schools. Among the artists represented are :
Spanish : Goya, El Greco, Murillo, Valdez. **Dutch :**
Rembrandt, Hals, Flinck, van de Velde. **Italian :** Titian,
Canaletto, Tintoretto, Fra Angelico, Bellini, Correggio.
Flemish and German : Rubens, Van Dyck, Breughel,
Faber. **English :** Turner, Constable, Romney, Stubbs,
Gainsborough, Reynolds, Hogarth. **French :** Millet, Corot,
Tissot, Daubigny, Monet, Delacroix, Degas, Poussin. **Irish :**
Jack B. Yeats, Sir William Orpen, Nathaniel Hone, Walter
Osborne and Sir John Lavery.

The gallery incorporates a national portrait section, and
there is also an excellent restaurant in the building.
Hours of opening : Weekdays 1000 to 1800. Sundays
1400 to 1700. Late night opening, Thursday, to 2100
Free Valuation : Each Thursday from 1030 to 1230, a
member of the staff is available to identify and value
paintings
Lectures : There are free lectures on art at the National
Gallery during weekday lunch-hours and at some other
times

The Municipal Gallery of Modern Art, Parnell Square,
Dublin 1. Tel. 41903

Founded by Sir Hugh Lane in 1907, the gallery is now
based in Charlemont House, designed and built by William
Chambers in 1765. It is intended that the Municipal Gallery will eventually transfer its European collection to the
National Gallery, and expand its own collection of Irish

paintings. Because suitable premises were not available for his own collection, Sir Hugh Lane lent his pictures to the National Gallery in London. When he was drowned on board the *Lusitania* in 1915, a codicil to his will bequeathing the works to the Municipal Gallery was held invalid since it lacked the technical requirement of two witnessed signatures. A compromise was reached in 1959, and the 39 pictures were divided into two collections, to alternate at five-yearly intervals between Dublin and London. Among the paintings in the gallery are works by Monet, Bonnard, Boudin, Corot, Renoir, Ingres, Augustus John, Hone, Lavery and Orpen. The sculpture includes works by Rodin, an Epstein head of Lady Gregory, and a large number of works by Irish sculptor Andrew O'Connor. There are lectures on Irish art, admission free, at noon on most Sundays during the year.

Hours of opening : Tuesday to Saturday inclusive 1000 to 1800. Sundays 1100 to 1400. Closed on Mondays and bank holidays

PRIVATE GALLERIES

Agnew Somerville Gallery :
Molesworth Street, Dublin. Tel. 61587/88
Monday to Friday 1000 to 1800. Saturday 1000 to 1300

Carmel Galley :
8 Sth Great George's Street, Dublin 2. Tel. 774282
Monday to Friday 0900 to 1730; Wednesday half-day;
Saturday 0900 to 1800

Davis Gallery :
Capel Street, Dublin. Tel. 48169
Monday to Friday 0900 to 1730. Saturday 1000 to 1300

Dawson Gallery :
4 Dawson Street, Dublin 2. Tel. 776089
Monday to Friday 1000 to 1230; Saturday 1000 to 1300

David Hendriks Gallery :
119 St Stephen's Green, Dublin 2. Tel. 756062
Monday to Friday 1000 to 1800; Saturday 1000 to 1300

Project Gallery :
31 Lower Abbey Street, Dublin 1. Tel. 40282
Monday to Friday 1000 to 1730; Saturday 1000 to 1400.

Neptune Gallery :
122A St Stephen's Green, Dublin 2. Tel. 754190
Monday to Friday 0930 to 1330 and 1445 to 1730;
Saturday 0930 to 1300.

Oriel Gallery :
17 Clare Street, Dublin 2. Tel. 63410
Monday to Friday 1000 to 1730; Saturday 1000 to 1300

For Art Galleries in central Dublin *see* **Map** pp. 45-48.

MUSIC

It is indeed ironic that though music is probably the best
supported of all the arts in the city, there is not one single
concert hall, nor even the likelihood of one in the near
future; plans of the long-promised John F. Kennedy Hall
gather dust on the architect's drawing board waiting for
funds from the government. However, if you are prepared
to put up with such minor inconveniences as bad acoustics,
you have the opportunity of hearing a lot of music in
Dublin. There are a number of orchestras and opera and
choral societies, professional and amateur, and the local
talent is augmented by an increasing number of visiting
artistes.

Opera
   The *Dublin Grand Opera Society* has two seasons, in the
spring and winter each year, of Italian and German opera,
with visiting international artistes taking the leading roles.
Performances are in the Gaiety Theatre. The very professional *Rathmines and Rathgar Musical Society* is in fact

amateur, and presents a number of light operas, operettas and musicals each year at the Gaiety Theatre.

Classical Music

The *Radio Telefís Éireann Symphony Orchestra (R.T.E.S.O.)* gives a season of recitals on Sunday nights at 2000 at the Gaiety Theatre, with guest soloists and conductors. Tickets are always hard to come by. The *RTE Light Orchestra* concentrates on broadcasting, but occasionally gives free concerts in St Francis Xavier Hall on Friday evenings. The *New Irish Chamber Orchestra (N.I.C.O.)* gives regular recitals in Dublin and throughout the country, maintaining a high standard of performance. There are also two amateur orchestras, the *Dublin Symphony Orchestra,* and the *Dublin Orchestral Players.* The *Royal Dublin Society* organises a season of music recitals with Irish and continental artistes at their premises in Ballsbridge, and the very progressive *Limerick Music Association* often shares its visiting performers with a Dublin audience, usually at the Player-Wills Theatre, South Circular Road. Other concert venues are the Rupert Guinness Hall, and the Examination Hall, Trinity College. The French, German and Italian Cultural Institutes, and some other embassies, are bringing an increasing number of high calibre foreign musicians to Dublin for concerts. For mid-day music, *Trinity College Chapel,* and *St Anne's,* Dawson Street, often have free lunch-time organ recitals. Full details of concerts and recitals can usually be found in the daily newspapers or in *Counterpoint,* the monthly magazine of the Music Association of Ireland.

For other music *see* **Entertainment Pubs.**

MUSEUMS

The National Museum, Kildare Street, Dublin 2. Tel. 65521

Divided into three sections, Irish Antiquities, Art and Industrial, and Natural History (which is entered from Merrion Street), the National Museum was opened in 1890, and much of the original collection was made up of bequests from the Royal Irish Academy, the Royal Dublin Society and Trinity College. The National Antiquities section comprises the finest collection of early European Christian art, and among the most impressive pieces are the Ardagh Chalice, the Cross of Cong and the Tara Brooch. The Natural History section has a complete collection of Irish fauna, a good collection of bird life and three skeletons of the prehistoric giant Irish deer, known as the Irish elk. A serious shortage of funds, space and staff has resulted in a number of the exhibits being displayed badly or not at all. In recent years, the attention of the government, which is responsible for the Museum's upkeep, has been drawn to the deteriorating conditions, but as yet to no apparent avail. Admission free.

Hours of opening : Tuesday to Saturday (and bank holidays) 1000 to 1700. Sundays 1400 to 1700. Closed Mondays.

The Dublin Civic Museum, South William Street, Dublin 2. Tel. 771642

Built in 1765 for the Society of Artists, it has at various times been used as the Municipal Council Chamber, the Court of Conscience (a debtor's court), the stable for the Dublin Fire Brigade, and the Supreme Court set up by the 1919 Dáil. Since 1953 it has housed a permanent exhibition of antiquarian and historical items relating to Dublin. Admission free.

Hours of opening : Tuesday to Saturday 1000 to 1800. Sundays 1100 to 1400. Closed Mondays.

Heraldic Museum, Dublin Castle, Dublin 2. Tel. 776831

Incorporated in the Genealogical Office, where the Chief Herald will trace your ancestral family for a fee which depends on the amount of research required, or provide you with your appropriate family coat of arms.

Hours of opening : Monday to Friday 0945 to 1300 and 1415 to 1645.

For museums in central Dublin *see* **Map** on following pages.

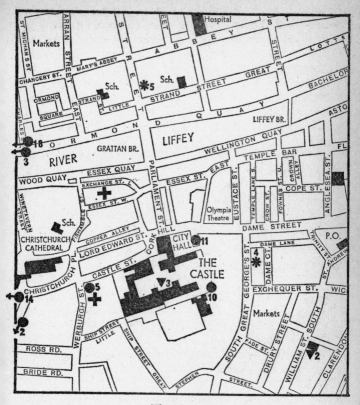

▼ **Museums**

2. Dublin Civic Museum	3. Heraldic Museum

* **Art Galleries**

4. Carmel Gallery	5. Davis Gallery

● **Places of Interest**

2. St Patrick's Cathedral	10. Dublin Castle
3. St Michan's Church	11. City Hall
5. St Werburgh's Church	14. Kilmainham Jail
	18. Four Courts

Map of Central Dublin showing Museums, Art Galleries and Places of Interest

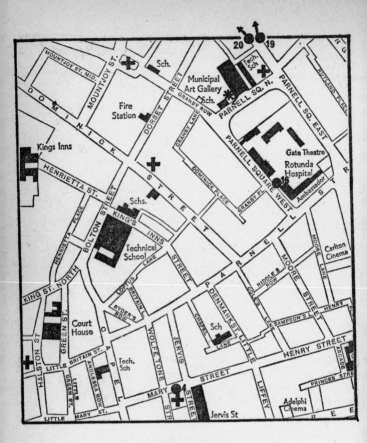

* Art Galleries

2. Municipal Gallery of Modern Art

● Places of Interest

4. St Mary's Church	19. Botanic Gardens
16. Rotunda Hospital Chapel	20. Phoenix Park

Map of Central Dublin showing Museums, Art Galleries and Places of Interest

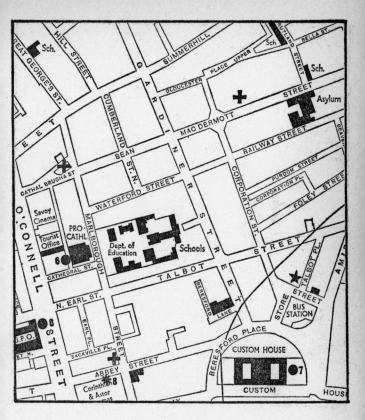

Map of Central Dublin showing Museums, Art Galleries and Places of Interest

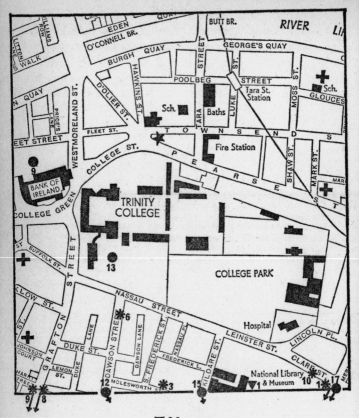

▼ Museums

1. National Museum

* Art Galleries

1. National Gallery of Ireland   8. Project Gallery
3. Agnew Somerville Gallery   9. Neptune Gallery
6. Dawson Gallery   10. Oriel Gallery

● Places of Interest

9. Bank of Ireland   15. Leinster House
12. The Mansion House   17. City Hall
13. Trinity College

Map of Central Dublin showing Museums, Art Galleries and Places of Interest

LIBRARIES

Trinity College Library, Trinity College, Dublin 2. Tel. 772941

The oldest library in Dublin, it began in 1601 with a collection of forty books. This number has now increased to over one million volumes, and by an act of 1801, the library is entitled to receive a copy of every book published in Britain or Ireland. Apart from the ancient Greek, Roman and Egyptian manuscripts, and a first edition of Dante's *La Divina Commedia*, the library houses the finest collection of early Irish manuscripts, and the centre-piece of the collection is the eighth-century Book of Kells, the most striking example of an illuminated manuscript of the period. Other volumes include the Book of Durrow, the Book of Armagh and the Book of Leinster, and there is a volume of letters of Queen Elizabeth I, individually signed, relating to affairs in Ireland from 1565 to 1570.

Hours of opening: Monday to Friday 1000 to 1700. Saturday 1000 to 1300. Closed Sundays and bank holidays.

National Library of Ireland, Kildare Street, Dublin 2. Tel. 65521 or 65524

The largest public library in Ireland, the National was founded in 1877, and contains a collection of about half a million volumes. The Irish historical and literary manuscripts, and the collection of Irish newspapers are useful for research and a microfilm service is available. The National Library, however, shares the same problem as the National Museum : shortage of space prevents the full collection from being available, and in fact a large quantity of volumes are stored at various depots throughout the city. Shortage of staff results in the library being closed completely between mid-July and mid-August—a particular inconvenience for foreign visitors.

Hours of opening: Monday to Friday 1000 to 2200. Saturday 1000 to 1300. Closed Sundays and bank holidays

Royal Irish Academy Library, Dawson Street, Dublin 2. Tel. 62570

Houses Irish historical manuscripts including the Book of Dun Cow, the Book of Ballymote, and an original autograph copy of the Four Masters. The library is closed for the last three weeks of August, and from 1230 to 1330 during July, August and September.

Hours of opening: Monday to Friday 0930 to 1730. Saturday 0930 to 1245.

Marsh's Library, St Patrick's Cathedral, Dublin 8. Tel. 753917

The oldest public library in Ireland, it was founded in 1707 by Narcissus Marsh, Archbishop of Dublin, and contains over 25,000 volumes mainly on medicine, theology, Hebrew, Greek, Latin and French literature. The cages in which readers were locked to prevent theft still remain.

Hours of opening: Monday 1400 to 1600. Closed on Tuesdays. Wednesday to Friday 1030 to 1230, 1400 to 1600. Saturday 1030 to 1230.

Chester Beatty Library, 20 Shrewsbury Road, Ballsbridge, Dublin 4. Tel. 692386

The most valuable and complete private collection of oriental manuscripts in the world. Included are manuscripts of the New Testament, Manichean papyri, illuminated Korans from different Islamic countries, and Arabic, Persian, Indian and Turkish manuscripts collected by the late Sir Alfred Chester Beatty.

Hours of opening: Monday to Friday 1000 to 1300; 1430 to 1700. Saturday 1500 to 1800. Closed Sundays and bank holidays.

Central Catholic Library, Merrion Square, Dublin 2. Tel. 61264

Contains 50,000 volumes on various subjects related to religion including a section on Christian art.

Hours of opening: Lending library: Monday to Friday

1200 to 2000. Saturday 1200 to 1600. Closed Sundays
Reference library : Monday to Saturday 1100 to 2200.
Sundays 1400 to 2200.

Irish Central Library for Students, 53 Upper Mount Street,
Dublin 2. Tel. 61167
Contains 50,000 volumes, mainly specialised books of
an educational nature.
Hours of opening : Monday to Friday 0930 to 1700 (1730
on Mondays). Closed for lunch 1300 to 1415.

Municipal Libraries
Dublin Corporation maintains 17 libraries in the city
and suburbs, with **Pearse Street** (tel. 771625) as the central
library.

LITERARY DUBLIN

Bernard Share

LITERARY Dublin is not what it was. But then, of course,
it never was. Hungry generations tread one another down,
reviling or reliving the past. Patrick Kavanagh is no longer
a presence in McDaid's, and the only echo is that made by
the new crowd jumping on his bandwagon. The Bailey,
in its latest manifestation as a haven for overheated expense
accounts, attempted to refuse admission to the president of
the Irish Book Publishers' Association, who was not wear-
ing the correct middle-class uniform. Literature has become
big business, sponsored by insurance and brandy and be-
dazzled with awards like a Ruritanian major's bosom.
Nobody is complaining, least of all the writers who, for
the first time in perhaps a thousand years, find themselves
courted rather than castigated. And they don't even always
have to wear collars and ties.
    You can go looking for them, if you like, in the pubs

51

and the poetry readings and the parties. But poetry is not produced over pints—would that it were; and the serious novelist slumped in a snug is fairly self-consciously off duty. There are still plenty of would-be writers, as there always were, but listening to one of them is rather like suffering the recounted seductions of a lounge-bar Casanova. The Dublin writer nowadays is as likely to put in his day in a government office as in a dockside shebeen, and Merrion Square is strictly for the birds. No Yeatses pace its pavements; no George Moore's lurk in developer-ravaged Hume Street: Dublin has outgrown itself, and the typewriters tinkle at least as actively in the faceless outer suburbs as amongst the retreating Georgian façades. All very sad, if you have a mind to drop a tear into the melting snows of yesteryear, but all perfectly logical. Literary Dublin, like musical Vienna or lascivious Paris, was only ever a wart on the face of an otherwise indifferent city. Mention Joyce and it was the brother that was remembered. Kavanagh was kicked around until he dignified himself in death. Literature, thank God, is not something you can get the whole populace hooked on like nicotine or alcohol or detergents—or even politics. Listen in the average pub and it's not Beckett you'll hear them discussing, but football or car performances or even, if you're unlucky enough, business. There are few writers nowadays who could parade themselves down Grafton Street with the certainty of being instantly recognised, as could Gogarty or Yeats or Behan. Not unless, that is, they had just appeared on television.

Yet Dublin, for its size, is a city suppurating with the printed, and the spoken, word. There is no shortage of people who write, or who think they can write but write all the same, and no lack of the peculiarly bitter vindictiveness that is the mark of a creatively-conscious community. We do a steady export trade in poets and novelists to the United States and beyond, most of whom return to enlarge, in several senses, on their experience. We have our Nobel man in Paris, an Ambassador-Poet in India. The British stage-Irish stamping ground is parochial and old hat. Irish literature, with Yeats in German, Aidan Higgins in umpteen languages, and Irish-language writers in Japanese, has spread its wings. The heady foreign airs blow across the Dublin literary scene, and the home-based writers sit in the corners of the new plush pubs and argue over percentages.

For the visitor, of course, this is so much water under the bridge. Dublin still has its literary ghosts, is still compact enough and, in spite of the grey flannel vandals, sufficiently homogeneous to hold the image of vanished greatness. Mind you, you may have to penetrate to the suburbs to pick up a scent which has gone cold in the centre. Many of Joyce's landmarks have been obliterated, but the Beckett country still lies almost untouched alongside the abandoned Harcourt Street railway line, and Donleavy's dismal suburbs are still redolent with the scent of generations of rashers and eggs. Thanks to an odd time-warp there is as much of Swift and Mangan, Goldsmith and Sheridan as there is of Joyce or even Behan. The banks of the Royal Canal are earmarked for an autobahn, but Trinity—though vandalising itself in its own academic way—and St Patrick's still smell like the seventeenth century and James Clarence Mangan's jerky shade still twitters in dark corners. A first list, from memory, produced a round score of literary figures with secure Dublin connections, all of whom would rate some kind of marking in an international recognition test. There are plaques or statues to pinpoint some of them: Shaw and Wilde, Davis and Goldsmith, even Tom Moore at the meeting of the waters, *Fir* and *Mná*. There is no plaque, however, out in Santry, legendary home of the almost legendary Myles na gCopaleen, and James Stephens, whose blood was pure Liffey water, is oddly unremembered.

'I was born', said Stephens 'into the outskirts of a city that was packed with horses, packed with birds, packed with donkeys and goats, and packed with the living noises of these and of ten times more than these.' The nature of the packing has changed, but Dublin is still a city coagulated with self-expression, and if good talk does not make good literature, it can get a man off to a flying start. As a visitor, you can pick up a hint that will set you off, as likely as not, on your own chosen literary pilgrimage, for one fault that the Dublin literary world does not fall into is that of fashion. You can always find a champion ready to stand up for the very Irish writer you believe to be unfairly disregarded: Francis Stuart, AE, William Allingham, Eimar O'Duffy, Maria Edgeworth. Just drop a stone into the right pool and you will almost certainly provoke a ripple, because although Dubliners do not talk as consistently about literature as they are said to have done once, they most of them still know what they like, as against what they are told to like by the TV commercials. American bookmen are green with envy over the space we allow ourselves in the newspapers and periodicals to castigate one another's literary output. And a fair amount of this rubs off on the mythical man in the street.

There used to be an identifiable kind of Dublin writer— identifiable by the fact that he did not live in Dublin, or even in Ireland. There are still those who protest that they cannot live and work in the city, but literary exile these days, like economic exile, seems to be more a business of going and coming. The wanderers return to water their roots and you may catch one or two of them puzzledly trying to come to terms with the old city which is busy remaking itself in the image of Subtopia. You may also run into specimens of that even more exotic breed, the Bounty men, the 'international' (i.e., non-Irish) writers who have been lured here by the very real promise of tax remission on their literary earnings. It is too early yet to say whether these new invaders will meet the same fate as most of the others over the course of the centuries and become more Irish writers than the Irish writers themselves. If they do, then their next step will obviously have to be Joycean exile, which will bring us by a commodious vicus of recirculation back where we started. In the meantime, the Dublin literary scene (for most of them are to be found, off and on, in the capital) is peripherally enlivened. All we have to do now is to persuade them to publish their books here as well and Ir. Lit. will rate a quotation on the Stock Exchange.

Meanwhile, back among the crumbling slums, the stone squares pockmarked by new concrete, the pullulating pubs and the putrescent Liffey, the ghosts go on proving themselves to be forms more real than living man. Even though the house has been dutifully destroyed it is difficult to pass Eccles Street without sniffing for the smell of frying kidneys. You can still cross the street, with Beckett's Murphy, from Wynn's Hotel to Mooneys, both outwardly little changed. With Yeats in your head you can revisit the Municipal Galley and see it all through his myopically aristocratic eyes. There exists, allegedly, a diabolically executed piece of signwriting, executed—and that's the right word—by Brendan Behan not a thousand miles from Merrion Square. But we'll leave that one as a consolation prize for the thesis writers. The trouble is that after a few doses of this kind of thing you begin to forget whether you are tracking the authors or their characters, and it is easy to slip into the way of thinking of J. Joyce as a minor figure in a book by Leopold Bloom. Perhaps this is the true test of a 'literary city'—a place where the line between fact and fiction is never quite defined, a street or a pub or a park which exists always in double-focus, the image and the shade. One thing Dublin is not is a literary museum. There is little formal deference paid to past greatness, in spite of the odd plaque and statue, and nothing like Goethe's house or Shakespeare's second best bedroom. Only Joyce's tower, out in Sandycove, attains to the dignity of a one-man museum, and that, of course, is a monument not to Joyce, or even the brother, but to stately, plump, Buck Mulligan, yellow dressing-gown ungirdled, and to Kinch the fearful Jesuit.

You see?

ACCOMMODATION

BORD FÁILTE, the Irish Tourist Board, inspects, grades and registers hotels, motels and guest houses in Ireland, and a comprehensive list is published annually in an official guide, price 5p, which also gives the maximum price (excluding state tax and service charge) which a proprietor can charge for that particular year. Bord Fáilte also offers an international computerised Reservations Service enabling you to telephone the local tourist office, which checks the hotel and type of accommodation required and gives an answer to your inquiry within 15 seconds. Reservation inquiries made abroad are free, but there is a charge of 25p for reservations made in Ireland.

In Ireland	telephone	**Dublin** 781200
In U.K.	telephone	**London** 235-1200
		Manchester 766-1122
		Glasgow 332-9633
In U.S.	telephone	**New York City** 544-2448
		New York State 800-522-9610
		Washington D.C. 800-211-9460
		California 800-648-3000

Hotels are graded **A***, **A**, **B***, **B**, **C** and **D**. The top grade, **A***, is described by Bord Fáilte as 'Hotels which are particularly well equipped and furnished and offer a very high standard of comfort and service under widely experienced management and staff. A very high standard of cuisine is reflected in varied à la carte and table d'hôte menus. Night services are provided. Suites are available and most bedrooms have private bathrooms.' The lowest classification, Grade **D**, is described as 'hotels which are clean and comfortable but with limited facilities', and the other grades fall in between these two descriptions. In some cases the official description may be a little eulogistic particularly when applied to cuisine and 'night services', but by and large the list is dependable.

56

More serious is the apparent fact of hotel economics which require most of the large hotels, many of them in the Grade **A*** category, to provide services unconnected with the traditional business of running a hostelry. The presence of balls, dress dances, conventions and late-night hamburger bars often tends to create an atmosphere more akin to a busy railway station than a supposedly de luxe hotel. Because of this, visitors, particularly the elderly who may be presumed to require a greater degree of peace and quiet, might do better to stay in a smaller more intimate hotel, where the facilities are less ostentatious, but often as good and the price structure more inviting. There is also a good range of modern middle-priced hotels, such as the South County in Stillorgan or the P. V. Doyle chain of five hotels, where the single room nightly price ranges from about £1.50 in the low season to £2.50 in the high season.

The list which follows is a selection of the hotels in each category. The 1971 maximum price for a single room excluding breakfast (unless stated) is given, with the low season price (usually October to March) listed first.

Grade A*

Gresham, Upper O'Connell Street, Dublin 1. Tel. 46881. 220 rooms. **Price :** £2.75 and £5.25

Jury's, College Green, Dublin 2. Tel. 779811. 157 rooms. **Price :** £2.50 and £3.75

Intercontinental, Pembroke Road, Ballsbridge, Dublin 4. Tel. 67511. 314 rooms. **Price** (including bath) : £7.25 and £7.75

Russell, St Stephen's Green, Dublin 2. Tel. 754151. 57 rooms. **Price :** £2.25 and £5.00

Royal Hibernian, Dawson Street, Dublin 2. Tel. 772991. 117 rooms. **Price :** £2.25 and £4.75

Shelbourne, St Stephen's Green, Dublin 2. Tel. 66471. 172 rooms. **Price** (including bath) : £4.00 and £6.25

Grade A :

Clarence, Wellington Quay, Dublin 2. Tel. 776178. 70 rooms. **Price :** £1.87 and £2.50

Crofton Airport, Swords Road, Dublin 9. Tel. 373777. 93 rooms. **Price** (including bath) **:** £2.20 and £3.10

Green Isle, Naas Road, Clondalkin. Tel. 593406. 56 rooms. **Price** (including bath) **:** £1.30 and £2.40

Moira Hotel, Trinity Street, Dublin. Tel. 777328. 41 rooms. **Price :** £2.30 and £4.90

Montrose, Stillorgan Road, Dublin 4. Tel. 693311. 190 rooms. **Price :** £1.30 and £2.30

Powers Royal, Kildare Street, Dublin 2. Tel. 65243. 30 rooms. **Price** (including breakfast) **:** £2.75 and £3.88

Skylon, Upper Drumcondra Road, Dublin 9. Tel. 379121. 88 rooms. **Price** (including bath) **:** £1.50 and £2.60

South County, Stillorgan Road, Dublin 4. Tel. 881621. 70 rooms. **Price :** £2.50 and £4.00

Sutton House, Sutton. Tel. 322688. 22 rooms. **Price** (including breakfast) **:** £2.50 and £5.25

Wicklow, Wicklow Street, Dublin 2. Tel. 777939. 36 rooms. **Price** (including breakfast) **:** £3.00 and £4.00

Grade B*

Buswell's, Molesworth Street, Dublin 2. Tel. 64013. 64 rooms. **Price** (including breakfast) **:** £2.25 and £2.75

Lansdowne, Pembroke Road, Dublin 4. Tel. 62549. 29 rooms. **Price** (including breakfast) **:** £2.25 and £3.25

Lenehan, Harcourt Street, Dublin 2. Tel. 752043. 23 rooms. **Price :** £1.25 and £1.70

Mont Clare, Clare Street, Dublin 2. Tel. 62896. 30 rooms. **Price** (including breakfast) **:** £2.00 and £2.25

Grade B

Embassy, 35 Pembroke Road, Dublin 4. Tel. 684130. 10 rooms. **Price** (including breakfast) **:** £2.25 and £2.50

Northbrook, 22 Northbrook Road, Dublin 2. Tel. 65465. 16 rooms. **Price :** £1.30 and £1.50

Pelletier, 24 Harcourt Street, Dublin 2. Tel. 758876. 33 rooms. **Price** (including breakfast) **:** £1.50 and £2.00

Grade C

Fox's, 14 Lower Leeson Street, Dublin 2. Tel. 62660.
11 rooms. **Price** (including breakfast) : £1.50 and £1.75
Groome's, Cavendish Row, O'Connell Street, Dublin 1.
Tel. 45304. 10 rooms. **Price** (including breakfast) : £1.37
Morehampton, 21 Morehampton Road, Dublin 4.
Tel. 680718. 20 rooms. **Price** (including breakfast) : £1.75
and £2.00

Grade D

Parkway, 5 Gardiner Place, Dublin 1. Tel. 40469.
12 rooms. **Price** (including breakfast) : £1.50 and £1.62
Blossom's, 40 Parnell Square, Dublin 1. Tel. 45269.
17 rooms. **Price** (including breakfast) : £1.50 and £1.60

For flats (apartments) and hostels *see* **Students in Dublin**
pp. 112-120.

EATING IN DUBLIN

DESPITE the fact that the Irish are considered to be the
best fed nation in the world, Ireland is not particularly
noted for its gourmet food. Or perhaps it is because of
this fact; after all, if you are busy climbing the table of
the 'best fed nations' league', you cannot afford to spend a
great deal of time worrying about the niceties of haute
cuisine. Whatever the reason, we occupy a more humble
position in the 'best food' table. That is not to say that
there is no good food—smoked salmon, Dublin Bay
prawns, lobster, oysters and ham are among the Irish
specialities. Nor can one conclude that there are no good
restaurants in Dublin but merely that there are not enough
(certainly too few for a cosmopolitan capital city) and that
the ones which exist tend to be rather expensive.

To write a comprehensive good food guide requires a
palate educated by age, experience and travel, a great deal
of time, immense stamina and, most important, vast

amounts of money. Having none of these, I decided (reluctantly) not even to attempt such a task. Just as it would be most unfair to damn a restaurant on the strength of one or even a few samplings, it would be equally misleading to praise one on the basis of such limited research. What follows therefore is not a guide to good eating, though some of the establishments listed will undoubtedly provide this, but rather a guide to eating-houses in general. The establishment's name and address is given in all cases. The times of opening, last orders and telephone number are given where appropriate, and further comments and information where pertinent. To avoid unnecessary repetition I have divided the various eating establishments into different categories, but the services provided by each are not exclusive. For example, Bewley's Oriental Cafés provide tasty light lunches, but they are more widely known for their unique coffe-house atmosphere, and are therefore listed in the coffee-house section. Incidentally, the list is not exhaustive, and thus exclusion of a particular establishment should not necessarily be construed as condemnation.

HOTEL RESTAURANTS

The **Russell Hotel** restaurant, St Stephen's Green, tel. 754151, is open from 1230 to 1430 and 1830 to 2245. Average price for lunch is £3.30 including wine, and £4.00 for dinner with wine. This year as last it has been awarded a 2-star rating for outstanding cooking by the authoritative Egon Ronay Guide.

The **Gandon Restaurant**, Gresham Hotel, Upper O'Connell Street, tel. 46881, is open from 1230 to 1500 and 1830 to 2330. Lunch costs about £1.50 per person, and dinner about £1.75.

The **Shelbourne Hotel**, 27 St Stephen's Green, tel. 66471, has two restaurants with full licence; the main restaurant is open from 1230 to 1500 and 1830 to midnight, and prices average £1.25 for lunch and £1.75 for dinner. The hotel's very comfortable **Saddle Room** opens from 0715 to 1100 for breakfast, then from 1230 to 1500 and later from 1730 to 2330. Lunch costs about £1.50 and dinner £2.00.

In Dawson Street, the Royal Hibernian's **Lafayette Restaurant** tel. 772991, opens from 1230 to 2330 and costs approximately £2.50 for lunch and £3.00 for dinner. In the same hotel, the **Rotisserie** opens from 1200 to 2330 and charges about £1.75 for lunch and £2.00 for dinner.

In Ballsbridge, the Intercontinental Hotel's **Martello Roof Restaurant,** tel. 67511, is open from 1930 to 0030, except on Sundays, and dinner costs about £2.00.

Other good city centre hotel restaurants, where lunch costs about £1.00 and dinner about £1.50, are the new restaurant in the **Wicklow Hotel,** Wicklow Street, tel. 777939, **Powers Royal Hotel** in Kildare Street, tel. 65243, **The Four Courts Hotel** on Inns Quay, tel. 771161, the **Clarence,** Wellington Quay, tel. 776178, and **Buswell's Hotel** in Molesworth Street, tel. 64013, just a few yards from the entrance to Dáil Éireann. North of the city, there is the **Skylon Hotel,** Upper Drumcondra Road, tel. 379121, which is on the way to the airport, the **Marine Hotel** in Sutton, tel, 323613, one of the few hotels with a swimming pool, (but it is for club members and residents only) and the **Sutton House Hotel,** Sutton, tel. 322688, which has a very good table d'hôte dinner. On the south side the **Montrose,** tel. 693311, and the **South County,** tel. 881621, both on Stillorgan Road, as well as the **Tara Towers Hotel** on the Merrion Road, tel. 694666, are reliable and provide good value, and the restaurant in the **Royal Marine Hotel,** Dún Laoghaire, tel. 801911, which has an A* rating, is of a very high standard.

HAUTE CUISINE RESTAURANTS

The **Soup Bowl,** 2 Molesworth Place, Dublin 2, tel. 67649, has possibly the best reputation in town; small, intimate with excellent but expensive food. Open 2000 to 2400. It is necessary to book in advance.

It is also necessary to book in advance for **Snaffles**, 47 Lower Leeson Street, tel. 60790, which serves lunch from 1230 to 1430 at about £2.00 per person, and dinner from 1900 to 2300 at about £6.50 for two.

The **Ould Cod,** 1 Lincoln Place (near the rear entrance to Trinity College), tel. 64300, has dinner and dancing (to records and tapes) until 0100. The menu is relatively inexpensive and it is usually possible to have a light snack or hors d'oeuvres if you do not feel up to a main meal. They also serve an interesting lunch from Monday to Friday, again with records, jazz or rock, and the cost is about 65p.

The **Beaufield Mews,** Woodlands Avenue, Stillorgan, tel. 880375, serves dinner from 1830 to 2300 at about £1.75 a head. The dining-room furniture, the dinner service and even the cutlery are antiques, and for sale.

Another good out-of-town restaurant is the **Mirabeau,** Marine Parade, Sandycove, tel. 809873, where dinner from 1800 to 2330 costs about £5.00 for two.

Elephants, 109a Lower Baggot Street, tel. 67144, is a small intimate restaurant with pleasantly old-fashioned decor, open from 1830 to midnight. Dinner costs about £2.50 per person. One attractive feature of this restaurant is that you study the menu over an aperitif, in the elegant reception area, before ascending to the main restaurant.

The **Bailey,** 2 Duke Street, has a newly opened upstairs restaurant, with Victorian decor, tel. 773751, open 1830 to 2300. Dinner costs about £2.50 a head.

The **King Sitric**, on the East Pier in Howth, tel. 325235 or 324790, and open from 1830 to 2330 as well as Sunday lunch-time, specialises in sea-food, and dinner costs about £2.00 per person, and Sunday lunch 75p.

The **Old Dublin Restaurant,** 91 Frances Street, tel. 751173, open 1245 to 1430 and 1830 to 2300, has very good food, dinner at about £1.75; and in the same area, the **Lord Edward,** 23 Christchurch Place, Dublin 8, tel. 752557, is open till 2245 and has a special pre-theatre dinner at £1.55. Another very good restaurant is the **Bay-Leaf,** 41 Pleasants

Street, off Lower Camden Street, tel. 753257. Seating barely 20 people, it serves a good lunch for 60p and an excellent and reasonably priced dinner from 1800 to 2200 Tuesdays to Saturdays.

ETHNIC RESTAURANTS

Some of the best Italian food is served in the **Unicorn,** 11 Merrion Row, tel. 62182, which opens from 1230 to 1430 for lunch at about 75p and from 1830 to 2230 for dinner which costs about £1.50.

Nico's of 53 Dame Street, tel. 773062, is another good Italian restaurant as is **Bernardo's,** 19 Lincoln Place, tel. 62471, open 1200 to 1500 and 1800 to 0100.

There are a number of Oriental restaurants, the best being the **Golden Orient,** 27 Lower Leeson Street, tel. 62286, which opens from 1830 to 0100 and is closed on Sundays and bank holidays. Average cost of dinner is about £1.00.

The latest Chinese restaurant to open is the **Sunflower,** in Lower O'Connell Street, tel. 42363, which is very large and has the advantage of being air-conditioned. Open 1200 to 2400 on weekdays, 1300 to 2330 on Sundays.

Other Chinese restaurants are the **Chopstick,** 60/61 Dame Street, tel. 772049; the **Opal,** 112 Middle Abbey Street, tel. 40698; the **Universal,** 12A Wicklow Street, tel. 772580; the **Kum Tong** in Grafton Street, tel. 774031, and the **Luna** in Upper O'Connell Street, tel. 778473. All provide good value for money, and fast though rather brusque service. The prices in the **Chopstick** are slightly higher than the others, but the average price for a four-course set lunch served from 1200 to 1500, very popular on weekdays, is about 37½p. Dinner served up to 2330 and midnight on Saturdays, varies from 65p to £1.00 on average.

The only restaurant serving Pakistani food is the excellent but expensive **Tandoori Rooms,** attached to the **Golden Orient,** 27 Lower Leeson Street, which opens from 1900 to 0100. Average prices for dinner are £1.85 for table d'hôte and 85p for à la carte.

The **Calcutta Restaurant** and the **New Delhi Restaurant** in Camden Street, and the **Bombay,** 5 South Richmond Street, as the names suggest, serve Indian food (and European food as well) but the hottest curries are probably to be found in the **Taj Mahal,** 17 Lincoln Place.

PUB GRUB

Two pieces of yesterday's lightly-margarined bread wilting at the edges, enveloping a tiny piece of ham or processed cheese, and served with a cup of something only distantly related to coffee, is served at lunchtime to the mainly male clientele. For this you pay between 15p and 30p, salt and mustard provided free. Not all pubs are that bad; some offer toasted sandwiches, and bowls of soup; some even allow you to fumble over the tiny packet of butter to prove that they *do* use it, but there certainly is no tradition of providing the tasty pies and pastries and unlimited supply of pickles so common in English pubs.

If you want something more palatable, try **Davy Byrne's,** 21 Duke Street, for a hot pie or salad plate, good value though the drinks are expensive. **Neary's** in Chatham Street serves salads and oysters when they are in season. The **Stag's Head,** 1 Dame's Court, an old fashioned, popular and noisy pub at lunchtime, has a good hot lunch, usually beef or ham with a couple of vegetables, costing, with a glass of red wine, about 45p. Across the street, the smaller **Stag's Tail** also serves homely hot lunches, at about 35p a plate. **Bartley Dunne's,** 32 Lower Stephen Street, Dublin 2, serves excellent rolls and cheeses, and the candle-lit interior makes lunching something of an adventure. The **Bailey,** 2 Duke Street, has recently come under new management, and offers the best lunch-time food, but at night-time prices. **Searson's,** 42 Baggot Street, serves salad plates and oysters, and other suburban pubs such as the **Merrion** and the **Horse Show House** opposite the Royal Dublin Society showgrounds, have salads and steaks.

GRILL BARS

The **Shelbourne Grill,** entered from Kildare Street, is open from 1000 to 2300. The menu is good, draught beer available, and the service friendly. A light lunch or evening meal costs as little as 65p. Deservedly one of the most popular restaurants of its type it fills up quickly at lunch time and between 1800 and 1900. The only drawback is the ventilation, particularly when the room is crowded.

The **Bianconi Room,** in Dawson Street, is part of the Hibernian Hotel. Price and food range is similar to the **Shelbourne Grill,** though ventilation is even worse.

The Gresham Hotel's ultra-modern **Táin Grill Bar** in Upper O'Connell Street is excellent value; lunch and a glass of wine costs between 65p and £1.00—but, as with many Dublin eating establishments, there is always a queue to face between 1300 and 1330.

The **Embassy Grill** in the Intercontinental is more expensive; open from 0700 for breakfast, from 1230 to 1430 for lunch, and 1800 to 2200 for dinner; lunch costs about £1.50 and dinner about £2.00.

Across O'Connell Bridge on the north side of the River Liffey is **Daly's,** 10 Eden Quay. Noisy, unsophisticated, the set lunch at about 40p is good value, the steaks even better : for £1.00 you will get a huge steak covered with a mountain of vegetables and still have enough change for a pint; plain fare at its very best.

The **Berni Inn,** in Nassau Street, has four different restaurants similar to the Berni Inns in England. The steaks are dependably good, and there is an excellent salad bar in the basement.

COFFEE HOUSES

Pride of place goes to **Bewley's Oriental Cafés** in Westmoreland Street, George's Street and Grafton Street. The latter is the most fashionable and certainly the most crowded. **Bewley's** is one of the few remaining Dublin institutions, popular with a clientele ranging from elderly spinsters to young students, business executives to typists, and thankfully it has so far been preserved from modernisation. Open from 0900 to 1730 Monday to Friday, and 0900 to 1300 on Saturdays; breakfast, lunch and tea-time snacks are served, but it is the atmosphere and the coffee, cakes and buns (also sold over the counter) that attract the customers. Other coffee houses are colourless in comparison, though the **Tea-time Express** on the corner of Dawson Street and Duke Street, which serves and sells delicious cakes, comes a reasonable second.

Jonathan's, 39 Grafton Street, is trendy and particularly popular with au pairs and foreign students. Open from 0900 to 2400 on 6 days, from 1200 on Sundays, it serves coffees, light lunches (with interesting salads) at about 50p and has a wine licence. There is also a restaurant and discothèque downstairs, slightly more expensive, which is open till 0200.

The **Golden Spoon Restaurant** at 36 Grafton Street is similar to **Jonathan's** though less fashionable. Open 0930 to 0100 it serves coffees, lunches, dinner and has a wine licence.

The **India Tea Centre,** 21 Suffolk Street, is open from 1000 to 1915 and serves coffees, lunch at about 45p and high tea at 50p.

The **New Amsterdam** in South Anne Street (off Grafton Street) serves coffees and light meals, and opposite it the **Coffee Inn** serves good coffee, even better drinking chocolate and has a small menu of Italian dishes. It is one of the few places where you can eat a pizza in Dublin.

The **Inca Coffee House**, 18 Upper Merrion Street, has a traditional coffee-bar atmosphere, and is open from 1000 to 2330.

The numerous cafés in O'Connell Street have exotic names and good ice cream but there is little else to recommend them. They are noisy, garish and the food, though basic, is not as cheap as it should be. If you are in the O'Connell Street area and need a coffee it is more advisable to try one of the self-service restaurants attached to the cinemas, such as the Savoy or the Carlton, or one of the pubs nearby. In fact most Dublin pubs serve coffee though the quality varies a great deal.

MISCELLANEOUS EATING-HOUSES

Gaj's (pronounced 'guise') in Baggot Street is noisy, crowded and friendly; frequented mainly by students and the New Left, it is open till after midnight, and the menu includes such tasty snacks as sauerkraut, Hungarian goulash, and Welsh rarebit. A more settled clientele use the **Grey Door**, in Upper Pembroke Street, which serves a full breakfast from 0800, a business lunch from 1215, and in the evening a traditional Irish high tea which includes as much soda and brown bread as you can manage. Two other restaurants which specialise in good-value home-cooking are the **Alpha,** 37 Wicklow Street, open 0900 till 1900 and the **Hunting Horn,** 18 Merrion Row, open from 0900 to 1530. The **Connacht Restaurant,** 14 Dame Court, open till 2030 on weekdays, 1600 on Saturdays, has a good lunch for about 60p, with excellent gateaux and desserts. Service is fast and friendly. The **Olde Hob,** 48 Lower Leeson Street, is open 6 days a week from 1000 to 0100, serving coffee, lunch, light snacks and dinner. Carafe wine is good value; service very friendly.

LATE NIGHT EATING

The **Blue Caribbean,** 25 Lower Leeson Street, is open from 2000 to 0300 on weekdays and to 0200 on Sundays. There are a wine licence, good curry, and usually some music. **La Caverna,** 18 Dame Street, is also open till 0200, as is the downstairs restaurant in **Jonathan's** in Grafton Street. On weekdays, the **Golden Spoon Restaurant** in Grafton Street is open till 0100 and the **Paradiso,** 32 Westmoreland Street, till 0300. The **Kilimanjaro,** 142 Lower Baggot Street, is open till 0300 all week. **Jury's** has a restaurant for light meals, wine and draught beer served with meals, which is open till 0030 or 0100.

LATE-LATE NIGHT EATING

Still hungry at 0400? Well, the choice becomes more limited and you won't find anything which qualifies for the Michelin Guide, but the **Coffee Dock**, in the Inter-continental Hotel, Ballsbridge, has a 23-hour service, closing only between 0500 and 0600. The **Doon-A-Ri** on the Sandford Road in Ranelagh stays open till 0300 and 0500 at weekends, and at Kelly's Corner the **Manhattan** is open till at least 0400, usually much later. On the other side of the river is **Jacko's Steak House,** 3 Arran Quay, open from 2300 to 0500.

TAKE-AWAY FOODS

Shannon Foods, a caravan on the Merrion Road, operates 24 hours a day, serving hamburgers, hot dogs, chicken, minerals, etc. The **Great Wall,** 2c Main Street, Blackrock, tel. 882298, offers take-away Chinese food; it is open from 1200 to 1430 and 1700 to 2400 Monday to Friday, 1700 to 2400 on Sundays and 1700 to 0100 on Saturdays. The menu is as large as most Chinese restaurants, the service friendlier and the prices about the same. Telephone orders accepted. The **Mandarin,** 63 South Richmond Street, also has take-away Chinese food; open 1200 to 1430 and 1730 to 0030 on weekdays; on Fridays and Saturdays 1200 to 1430 and 1730 to 0130, on Sundays 1730 to 0030. **Punjab One,** on St Stephen's Green, has take-away Indian food. There are a number of other take-away food stores and mobile vans, serving fish and chips, hamburgers, hot dogs and fried chicken. In many cases the quality of food is poor; the standard of hygiene nightmarish.

CABARETS

Most of the cabaret in Dublin is home-grown, the population being too small to support top-flight international stars for more than a one-night concert. A number of hotels and pubs provide cabaret entertainment, usually on Saturday nights; there are, for example, the **Old Shieling**, Raheny, **Clontarf Castle**, Clontarf, **Clare Manor Hotel**, Coolock, and the **Green Isle Hotel,** Clondalkin. However, **Jury's Hotel, College Green,** provides all-the-year-round cabaret. From the end of April to mid-October there is an 'Irish cabaret' seven nights a week 2030 to 2300. A bit leprechaunish but harmless and popular. For the cabaret alone you pay about £1.50 which includes two drinks; if you are having dinner (à la carte menu) the cost of this is about 75p. During the autumn and winter, from Wednesday to Saturday, 2000 to 0100, there is dinner and dancing interspersed with cabaret spots, with the programme changing every two weeks. The cabaret adds about 75p to your bill. The **Clarence Hotel**, Wellington Quay, also has a summer cabaret, equally leprechaunish, but apparently it's what the visitors want.

DRINKING IN DUBLIN

Too much has been written about drink and the Irish, some of it true. I'll stick to the bare facts. The normal hours for pubs in Dublin on weekdays are from 1030 to 1430 and 1530 to 2330 in the summer (April to October) and to 2300 in the winter (November to March). The closed period between 1430 and 1530 is known as the 'holy hour', and does not apply to pubs outside Dublin and other major centres. For off-beat drinking hours, *see* **The Twenty-Four Hour Pub Crawl.** On Sunday, pubs are open from 1230 to 1400 and 1600 to 2200 throughout the year. St Patrick's Day follows the Sunday times, and all pubs are closed on Christmas Day. Hotel residents can order alcohol at any time, except on Good Friday when it can only be ordered with meals, and on Christmas Day when it is available from 1300 to 1500 and 1900 to 2200 only.

No pubs are barred to women though there is an unstated convention that women use the lounge bar if there is one. In the lounge section of a pub, incidentally, drinks cost at least 1p more per drink. Any pub can refuse a member of the public admittance or service, without offering any explanation. Drink is more expensive than in Britain, and prices tend to be revised annually in an upwards direction, though they are lower than in the U.S. and Scandinavia. There is no standardised price structure, and a pint of beer can vary in price from 17p to 25p in two pubs in the same neighbourhood. Only persons of 18 years of age or over may buy or be served alcohol in a public house.

BAD PUBS

No need to mention any names; they are in the majority and you will recognise them without any difficulty. The service is impersonal, the decor synthetic and the over-pricing all too real. There is, however, a school of thought which points out that any place which serves a drink cannot be all that bad.

GOOD PUBS

It is difficult to define what makes a good pub, since it is of course a matter of personal taste. I am told that some people actually enjoy sitting on mock-leather armchairs, in plastic-coated rooms lit by frosted glass coach-lamps, listening to wall-to-wall muzak. If you are of this persuasion, I regret to say that you have all too great a scope in Dublin. To me, however, a good pub is one that never forgets that its two most important services are drinking and conversation, in that order, and thus provides or preserves an ambience where these two ingredients may be enjoyed to the full, though not necessarily at the same time. Since there are over 700 pubs in the Dublin area, you may need some guidance :

A good example of what I mean is the **Palace Bar,** 21 Fleet Street (just off Westmoreland Street) : sombre, spacious, with a cosy snug and a very good pint. Off O'Connell Street, in Prince's Street at the entrance to the Capitol Cinema, is the **Prince's Bar,** only about 50 years old, but the mahogany, marble and mirrors give it a more traditional appearance. Behind Burgh Quay in Poolbeg Street is **Mulligan's,** one of the many Dublin pubs mentioned by Joyce; unlike some of the others, it has not traded on the Joycean connection but prospers by maintaining its traditional, simple character. It is frequented mainly by a young clientele. Merrion Row (about 100 yards past the Shelbourne Hotel in a southerly direction) has a number of interesting pubs mentioned in the other categories. One of the better ones is **Doheny & Nesbitt's,** usually called by the latter name, another example of a pub which has happily ignored the modernisation mania. The snug is comfortable, the bar isn't, but the furniture, wrought-iron tables, etc. is picturesque and the atmosphere lively. Fifty yards over Leeson Street Bridge on your left you will find **O'Brien's,** noisy, crowded, with a good pint —a plain man's pub and all the better for that. If you ask a Dubliner to recommend a really traditional pub, nine out of ten will lead you to the **Brazen Head,** the most traditional of all Dublin's taverns. Just off the quays on the South side of the river Liffey, at 20 Lower Bridge Street, the **Brazen Head** has been a pub for at least 300 years, and the dark smoky atmosphere and decor remain unchanged. The only snag is that draught beer and stout are not served. My own favourite pub is the **Long Hall,** 51 South Great George's Street, which leads into Dame Street. The glittering lights, mirrors, lamps, should classify it as kitsch(y), but somehow the whole mixture works, making it one of the most attractive pubs anywhere, with friendly efficient service, offering one of the best-pulled pints in town, and excellent thirteen-year-old whiskey from the cask.

ENTERTAINMENT PUBS

For traditional Irish music, **O'Donoghue's** of Merrion Row is undoubtedly the best. Crowded to capacity almost every night, there is no cover charge, the music is of a very high standard, but most important, it is authentic; here the musicians play for themselves and each other, the packed enthusiastic audience is only incidental. More commercial but still very good is the **Chariot Inn** in Ranelagh, which has folk ballads and occasionally an Irish play. If the singing becomes too noisy, you can escape upstairs to a luxuriously quiet lounge bar. Further afield there are the celebrated **Abbey Tavern** in Howth, the **Old Shieling** in Raheny, the **Purty Kitchen** in Dún Laoghaire, and the **Embankment** in Tallaght. There are in fact about two dozen bars, lounges and hotels which provide ballad sessions, particularly at summer weekends. The cover charge varies from about 30p to 50p and current details can be found in the evening newspapers. **Slattery's** of Capel Street has a more varied repertoire, catering for folk, ballads, blue grass and jazz on different nights. **Kelly's**, 50 Sir John Rogerson's Quay, specialises in jazz, and the **Coliemore Hotel**, Dalkey, usually has a jazz happening on Saturday or Sunday nights. The only drag show in town is done in the **Baggot Inn** in Merrion Row, called **Pussy's Parlour** after the resident artiste, Mr Pussy.

PROFESSIONAL PUBS

This category is for the people who like to meet and talk 'shop' in the evenings with the people they have met and talked shop with during the day. The upstairs lounge of the **Pearl Bar**, 37 Fleet Street, is the main meeting place for Dublin and visiting journalists. It is opposite the side entrance of the *Irish Times*, and free newspapers are provided. *Irish Press* journalists use the **Silver Swan**, 4 George's Quay. The television crowd use the **Merrion Inn** or the **Montrose Hotel** in Stillorgan. Actors naturally drink close by their theatre and the **Plough**, 28 Lower Abbey Street, directly opposite the Abbey Theatre, and **P. J. Molloy's,** 59 Talbot Street, are the main two. Wherever they are playing, most actors and their camp followers gravitate towards **Groome's,** 8 Cavendish Row, opposite the Gate Theatre, for a last drink, where they co-exist peacefully enough with the other main interest group, members of the Fianna Fáil party. The racing crowd use the **Old Stand,** 37 Exchequer Street, and the young sports-carred executives crowd into the **Wicklow Hotel,** in Wicklow Street. Poets and writers hold court in **McDaid's,** 3 Harry Street, off Grafton Street, and **Sinnott's,** 3 South King Street, which also caters for the dwindling number of Irish speakers. There is a bar in the **Four Courts** for barristers, and the **Four Courts Hotel,** 50 yards further down Inns Quay, is another popular meeting place for legal people. Advertising executives use the **Pembroke,** in Pembroke Street, and gravediggers drink in **Kavanagh's** beside Glasnevin cemetery.

THE 24-HOUR PUB CRAWL

Begin say at 1030 in any of the pubs mentioned in the Good Pub section. You should cover about half of them and have located some new ones by the time the 'holy hour' comes up at 1430. At this stage you can take a taxi (don't drive!) to the **Embankment, Lamb Doyle's** or another of the pubs outside the city which don't close for the 'holy hour', or try a restaurant or hotel for a quick lunch and bottle of wine, till 1530 when the pubs re-open. Finish off the Good Pub list and move on to the Professional Pub list till about 2000 when the entertainment pubs come alive. In the summer months you can continue your marathon until 2330. At this stage, you could order a couple of dozen bottles which the barman will wrap discreetly in a heavy brown paper bag, and follow the other people with brown paper bags to the inevitable post-pub party. Or again resort to a restaurant, where you must order your wine (beer and spirits rarely served) before 0030. When they throw you out, crawl or taxi back to your hotel and continue your vigil till 0645. Walk or stagger to the Markets area in the direction east of Capel Street, where at around 0700 you can help to open up the pubs which serve the workers in the fish, fruit and flower markets. Among them are **Keating's**, 51 Arran Street East, the **Market Bar**, Little Mary Street, or **Martin Hughes'**, 19 Chancery Street. Alternatively you could try one of the pubs such as **Galligan's** or **Mulvihill's** on the North Wall, which open at the same time for dockers on their way to work. After a couple of hours have a quick sauna bath and you should be ready for 1030 opening time again!

SHOPPING IN DUBLIN

GRAFTON STREET is the most fashionable (and expensive) shopping area in the city, but there are well-serviced areas, within easy walking distance, the main ones being Henry Street, O'Connell Street, and South Great George's Street. The normal shopping hours in the city are 0900 to 1730 or 1800, from Monday to Saturday, with a half day on either Wednesday or Saturday. All city centre shops are closed on Sundays and bank holidays.

HAUTE COUTURE

The leading Irish fashion designers are **Ib Jorgensen**, 25 Fitzwilliam Square; **Mary O'Donnell**, 43 Dawson Street, and **Wolfangel**, 60 Lower Baggot Street.

LARGE STORES

Switzer's and **Brown Thomas**, both of Grafton Street, are the leading department stores, both having the usual complement of women's, men's and children's departments, furniture, glass, gifts, toys, restaurants, cafés, hairdressers, public telephones, and information bureaux. **Arnott's** of **Henry Street** has all the usual departments of a large store including a restaurant, but **Arnott's** of **Grafton Street** concentrates on women's fashions. **Richard Alan** at the top of

Grafton Street, and **Colette Modes** of Grafton Street and South Great George's Street, are both popular for ladies' clothes, and **Cassidy's** of O'Connell Street has four floors of fashion fabrics including traditional Irish báinín and handwoven tweed. **Clery's** department store in O'Connell Street is also good for fabrics; and **Roches Stores** and **Penneys** in Henry Street are middle-priced department stores.

BOUTIQUES

Most of the boutiques cluster around the Grafton Street area. In the Grafton Arcade, two of the newer boutiques are **Ambush** and in the basement below, **Sundance**, which specialises in suede and leather handcrafts. At the top of Dawson Street, the very elegant **Anna Livia** specialises in Irish tweeds. In Duke Lane, off Duke Street, you will find **Un Coin de Paris** very French and expensive, and **It's a Beautiful Day,** which specialises in fun clothes and trendy gear. In Molesworth Street is **Pat Crowley**, where the emphasis is on handknits, crochets and accessories, and on the other side of Grafton Street, **Pia Bang**, 10 Johnstons Court, which sells the young French casual look. In Lower Leeson Street there is the Nigerian designer **Rufina**, in Ely Place you will find **Gilli**, in Merrion Row **Crow**, and at 20 Upper Baggot Street, **Open Til Eight**, which does just that, serves coffee, and occasionally opens on Sunday. In the George's Street area there is the up to the minute **Drury Lane Boutique** at 18 Drury Street, off Exchequer Street; **An Poc ar Buile,** 2 Fade Street, off South Great George's Street, which has a distinctly Irish flavour, concentrating on tweeds and wools, and **Rag Doll**, 24 Market Arcade, George's Street, with a mainly young clientele. Two out of town boutiques are **Le Tabard,** 61A Rock Road, Booterstown, which specialises in crochet, handknits and small articles of house furnishing such as lamps and batiks, and the **Mary Davies Boutique** in Enniskerry, thirteen miles from Dublin, which stocks the now world-famous Donald Davies, finely woven tweed fashions.

MEN'S FASHIONS

Both in range and price men's clothes in Dublin compare unfavourably with London and indeed with most European cities. Of the large department stores, **Brown Thomas** is the best for men's fashion; their **Mr. B. T. Boutique** is stylish though pricey. The London firm of **Austin Reed** has recently opened their first Irish branch at the top of Grafton Street, providing good quality, mostly Irish-made clothes, not to mention some long-overdue competition to the local outlets. In Duke Lane there are three boutiques. **Jeffson,** which has a good range of accessories such as hats and hand made boots, is undoubtedly the most fashionable. Opposite, **Adam** provides good continental style suits and jackets, mainly from Amsterdam, and these are less expensive. **Stephen Rondo** is particularly good for leather and suede. At the top of Grafton Street is **Tyson's,** the traditional and dependable 'Gentleman's Outfitter', and opposite, **F. X. Kelly,** good quality fashionable clothes with a very wide range of suits. In Westmoreland Street, **Kennedy and McSharry** and **Callaghan's** of Dame Street are both gentlemen's outfitters of the old school; **Woodrow's** of O'Connell Bridge House has a wide range of jackets and sweaters. Other men's shops are **Alan Mark's** in Exchequer Street, **Alan King,** Middle Abbey Street, **Ken Stuart Fashion,** Upper Liffey Street, and **Bests** of O'Connell Street. **Galligan's** of Henry Street has a very good range of sweaters; and along Capel Street there is a large number of clothes shops for younger men with the emphasis on price rather than quality. **O'Connor's** of Abbey Street stock the widest range of denims and levis, both for men and women.

IRISH GOODS/SOUVENIRS

You will find a wide range of quality Irish goods in the large department stores, particularly **Brown Thomas** and **Switzer's,** such as the world renowned Waterford glass, Irish pottery, linen, tweed and Aran sweaters. In recent years there has been a significant advance in the field of Irish design, and the use of traditional celtic motifs in a contemporary setting has been especially successful. This progress has been spearheaded by the government-sponsored Kilkenny Design Centre, and the products from these workshops are available in a number of Dublin shops. **Market Ireland** in Grafton Street has very good silver work, not too expensive, either, and Irish pottery and copperware. In Molesworth Street there is **Rionore** of Kilkenny which has exceptionally good handmade jewellery, and next door **Craftsmen Ltd,** which stocks the complete range of Kilkenny designed goods as well as the gold and silver work of other craftsmen. In South King Street you will find **Marika** who actually makes modern gold and silver jewellery on the premises according to her customers' specifications, so you are likely to get exactly what you want—and at a very reasonable price. One of Dublin's most popular craft shops is **Fergus O'Farrell** in Duke Street, where you can buy finely carved wooden figures and bronze work. In the Creation Arcade, the **Donegal Shop** and **Creation Boutique** have a good range of Irish tweed and traditional Aran sweaters, and in Duke Lane in the **Weaver's Shed,** you can actually see the weaving in progress. In Dawson Street, **Irish Cottage Industries** is also very good for tweeds and you will find Connemara handmade tweeds in **Miller's** of 31 Nassau Street and Clifden, Connemara; they also have household goods, silver work, toys, patterns and crochet work. Also in Nassau Street, **Kevin and Howlin** specialise in Irish tweeds.

For souvenir-style souvenirs, a number of city centre shops stock the usual clocks, table mats and scarves, but look out for the words '*déanta sa tSeapáin*' which simply means that your ethnic Irish-style ashtray or piece of turf is in fact made in Japan. You could do worse than order a plaque with your family crest or coat of arms; if your name is Murphy most souvenir shops can oblige. For the Kowouskis and Silversteins with Celtic hangups, try one

77

of the specialists, such as **Heraldic Artists Ltd,** 9A Trinity Street, or **Mullin's of Dublin,** Heraldic House, 36 Upper O'Connell Street.

ANTIQUES

Despite the number of antique shops—there are over 50 in Dublin alone, not to mention a 30-stall antique Hyper-market—Irish antique prices are rather high, and in fact a growing number of dealers are travelling to England to buy their antiques. Most of the antique shops are situated between Kildare Street and South William Street; few dealers concentrate exclusively on one particular type of antique, though many have a particular interest or speciality. At 19 Kildare Street you will find **Kildare Antiques;** good for eighteenth-century porcelain and Belleek China, and also in Kildare Street, **R. McDowell,** for eighteenth-century furniture. In Molesworth Street there are **Jane Williams Antiques** for Georgian furniture and **Anthony Antiques. Dooly's** of 29 Dawson Street have Irish and English period furniture, as do **City Antiques,** 3 Dawson Street. **Bernard Antiques** are in Duke Street, and also in the lower ground floor of Brown Thomas; in South Anne Street there is **H. Danker, John O'Reilly's Fine Art Showrooms** and **J. W. Weldon,** also of 55 Clarendon Street, for eighteenth-century silver and Victorian jewellery. Nearby, at 45 Clarendon Street, there is an antique shop with a difference, the **Carmelite Mission Shop** which operates with a narrower profit margin, and all proceeds go to the foreign missions. In South William Street are the **Georgian Shop** and **Kenyon Antiques,** with early Georgian and Queen Anne furniture. In Grafton Street, **Louis Wine** has more antique Irish and English silver than you are likely to see anywhere in these islands. The **Dandelion Green** in St Stephen's Green, near the top of Grafton Street, usually has between 20 and 30 antique boutiques, with everything from Victorian bric-à-brac to objets d'art. There are a number of interesting antique shops and auction rooms along the Quays, including **Edwards Butler,** 14 Bachelor's

Walk, and **Orken's,** 32 Ormond Quay. Out of the city centre, you will find **Eibhlin Spain,** 16 Sandford Road, Ranelagh, which has some very fine period furniture. The annual Irish Antique Dealers' Fair is held in the Mansion House, Dawson Street, each June.

PAINTINGS, PRINTS, COINS & STAMPS

The **Carmel Gallery,** South Great George's Street, **Combridges** of Grafton Street and the **Grafton Gallery** in Harry Street all have a good range of reasonably priced watercolours and oils. The **Godolphin** in Nassau Street, the **Oriel Gallery** in Clare Street, the **Dawson Gallery** in Dawson Street and the **Agnew Somerville** in Molesworth Street have good period oil paintings, and they and the other galleries listed in the Art section have regular exhibitions of contemporary Irish painters and will put you in touch with their artists.

The **Neptune Gallery** specialises in rare prints and a very wide range of low-priced engravings is provided by **Historic European Artists,** ranging from political cartoons to topographical views to rare newspapers. Their main outlet is **Switzer's** of Grafton Street.

Kevin O'Kelly, 21 Wellington Quay, has a large range of old coins, medals and medallions; other numismatists are **I & G Coin,** 41 Leopardstown Drive, Blackrock, Co. Dublin, **Numismatic Depot,** 19 Merrion Row, and **Margaret Kiely,** 35 Sycamore Road, Finglas, Dublin 11.

For stamp collectors : **David Feldman,** 102 Leinster Road, Dublin 6 are specialists in the philately of Ireland, and **A. L. Stokes,** 25 Pembroke Park, Ballsbridge, is secretary of the Dublin Philatelic Club.

BOOKS

Antiquarian

The main antiquarian booksellers who will buy as well as sell rare books are the **Museum Bookshop,** 35 Kildare Street, which deals in rare maps and prints; **James O'D**

Fenning, 11 Osborne House, Seapoint Avenue, Seapoint; **Hodges Figgis,** Dawson Street; **Fred Hanna,** Nassau Street and **Carraig Books,** 25 Newtown Avenue, Blackrock.

Bookshops

Eason's of O'Connell Street is a vast store, stocking books of all kinds, as well as stationery and national and foreign newspapers and magazines. The **University Bookshop Hodges Figgis,** 5/6 Dawson Street, which is over 200 years old, stocks a wide range of specialised and general interest books, and they have a special **Celtic Studies** branch on the opposite side of the street. Also in Dawson Street are **Browne & Nolan's,** with a good religious and educational department, and the **A.P.C.K.** which is particularly good for children's books. Another bookshop with a good religious department is **Gill's,** 50 Upper O'Connell Street. The **Paperback Centre** in Suffolk Street has an excellent classics, poetry and plays section, and operates a mail order service within the Republic. The **Eblana Bookshop,** at the top of Grafton Street, is a general bookstore with very helpful service and the best of the work of Ireland's smaller poetry presses. **New Books,** 16a Pearse Street, specialises in socialist and communist literature. Out of town, there are the **Paperback Centre** and the **Book Centre** in the Stillorgan Shopping Centre, and **Parsons** on Baggot Street Bridge.

Second-hand Books

Fred Hanna of Nassau Street buys and sells second-hand books, and is particularly good for school and university text books. **Green's,** 16 Clare Street, have second-hand books, starting as low as 5p, and a selection is usually on display in stalls on the pavement outside. Along the quays, **George Webb,** 5 Crampton Quay, and the **Dublin Bookshop,** 32 Bachelor's Walk, have a good range of second-hand books, providing hours of pleasant browsing on a Saturday afternoon.

TRANSPORT

AIRPORT

Dublin Airport (Collinstown), tel. 370191, is 6 miles north of the city centre. The city air terminal is at **Busarus,** Store Street, tel. 42941, and special airport buses depart approximately every 20 minutes. The fare is 30p for adults, 12p for children. The 41A bus from Lower Abbey Street (between O'Connell Bridge and Butt Bridge) will bring you within ¼ mile of the airport at less than half the price. The airport restaurant has a fairly high reputation, and there are the usual cafeterias, bars, shops and bank. There are direct flights to most centres in the United Kingdom, to Europe and the United States. Taxis to and from the airport should cost about £1.00.

AIRLINE OFFICES

Aer Lingus (Irish International Airlines): 40 Upper O'Connell Street, Dublin 1, 42 Grafton Street, Dublin 2, and 12 Upper George's Street, Dún Laoghaire.

Travel in Ireland and to U.K.: tel. 377777; international flights: tel. 377747. Flight enquiries: tel. 370191

Air Canada : 4 Westmoreland Street, Dublin 2. Tel. 771488

Air France : 1 Westmoreland Street, Dublin 2. Tel. 779073

Alitalia : 60/63 Dawson Street, Dublin 2. Tel. 775171

B.E.A : 38 Westmoreland Street, Dublin 2. Tel. 772821

BOAC : 112 Grafton Street, Dublin 2. Tel. 778261/3

British United Airways : Aer Lingus are the agents.

Iberia : 3 Grafton Arcade, Grafton Street, Dublin 2. Tel. 774368

K.L.M : Hawkins House, Hawkins Street, Dublin 2. Tel. 778241

Lufthansa : Unity Buildings, 16 Lower O'Connell Street, Dublin 2. Tel. 47751

North East Airways : Aer Lingus are the agents.

Pan American World Airways : 26 Westmoreland Street, Dublin 2. Tel. 779091

S.A.S : 53 Middle Abbey Street, Dublin 2. Tel. 43346
Sabena : 109 Grafton Street, Dublin 2. Tel. 773440
Swissair : Grafton Buildings, 34 Grafton Street, Dublin 2.
Tel. 778173
T.W.A : 44 Upper O'Connell Street, Dublin 1. Tel. 45651

AIRCRAFT HIRE

Iona National Airways, Cloghran, Co. Dublin. Tel 378323/
375228/27990, ext. 699. Outside office hours : 300888. Two
Cessna 172 single-engine 3-passenger aircraft for internal
flights at about £15.00 per hour. Cessna 310 twin-engine
5-passenger aircraft for internal, U.K., Europe and N.
Africa flights at about £35.00 an hour.

Ireland West Airways, at Dublin and Castlebar airports.
Scheduled services to Shannon, Kerry, Galway and Mayo,
and charters to Europe.
West Coast Office, tel. Castlebar 448 or Castlebar 99.
East Coast Office, tel. Wicklow 0404. Telex 5474.

HELICOPTER HIRE

Irish Helicopters Ltd, 3a Clyde Road, Ballsbridge, Dublin
4. Tel :689761/683776. Outside office hours tel : 689761.
4-seater Alouette II at £70.00 an hour and 6-seater
Alouette III at £95.00 per hour.

BICYCLE HIRE

The second cheapest form of travel and particularly useful
to beat the rush-hour traffic, bicycles can be hired at a
number of city shops, under the Irish Raleigh Rent-a-Bike
Scheme. The cost is approximately 40p a day, or £2.50 a
week, though there is a refundable deposit of between
£2.00 and £5.00 to be paid. The scheme operates from
April to September only.

Among the shops are :
R. W. Stevens Ltd, 169 Pearse Street. Tel. 778009
R. W. Stevens Ltd, 27 Bachelor's Walk. Tel. 43826

McHugh Himself, 39 Talbot Street. Tel. 46694
Eltoy Ltd, 38 Mary Street. Tel. 40556
Charleys, 35 Ballybough Road. Tel. 44090
Fagan's, 46a Capel Street.

CRUISER HIRE

Irish Hire Boat Operators, 23 Clyde Road, Dublin **4. Tel. 680674. Charter Boats Association of Ireland,** 18 Berkeley Street, Dublin 7. Tel. 301511

These two firms are associations for a number of cruiser hire firms throughout Ireland. The nearest moorings to the city are at Lucan, Co. Dublin, but most cabin cruisers are berthed on the river Shannon, which offers the very fine boating facilities and the wide open spaces that can no longer be found in England. The hire charge in April and October is almost exactly half the charge of the peak period summer months. **4-berth cabin cruiser :** £32.00 in April and October, £66.00 in August (approx). **6-berth cabin cruiser :** £45.00 in April and October, £85.00 in August (approx).

CARAVAN HIRE

The average rate for a fully-equipped caravan in the summer ranges from £12.50 a week for a 4-berth caravan to £17.00 a week for a 6-berth caravan.

Caravans can be hired from :
Green Isle Caravans, Clonkeen Road. Tel. 895427
Irish Caravan Service, 26 Fitzwilliam Square. Tel. 65057
Malcolms Caravans Ltd, 7a Ranelagh Road. Tel. 975713
Young Caravans, 1 Ballytore Road. Tel. 908993 and **Rentasprite,** see below.

CARAVAN SITES

Cromlech Cottage Caravan and Tent Park, Killiney Hill Road, near Ballybrack. Tel. 804562
Rentasprite, Sherrindon Park, Shankill, Co. Dublin. **Tel.** 863006

HORSE-DRAWN CARAVANS

They are usually associated with the Ring of Kerry; although they cannot be hired in Dublin, you can hire one in Co. Wicklow. The rate varies with the season; a 4-berth caravan, fully equipped with linen, cooking equipment and tableware will cost about £15.00 a week in the off season and about £35.00 in the summer months. 5-berth caravans range from about £20.00 to £40.00 a week. They are available from :

Bray Caravan Co., 73 Main Street, Bray, Co. Wicklow. Tel. 897601

Horseshoe Caravans, Kilmanagh, Glenealy, Co. Wicklow. Tel. 0404-8188

CROSS-CHANNEL BOATS

Dublin–Liverpool B+I Motorway, 16 Westmoreland Street, Dublin 2. Tel. 777345. Enquiries between 0700 and 0900, tel. 41185. Departure is from the Ferryport, Dublin 1; passage is by modern 'drive-on' car ferry throughout the year; in winter there is a sailing every day except Saturday, and during the summer there are day and night sailings in each direction daily on weekdays, and thrice-daily sailings at weekends. Length of the voyage is $6\frac{3}{4}$–7 hours. Berths available.

Fares :

Passenger accompanying car, single fare £2.80 each (approx). Passenger without car, single fare £4.00 each (approx).

Dún Laoghaire–Holyhead British Rail, 15 Westmoreland Street, Dublin 2. Tel. 42931. Emergency calls after hours, tel. 801905 (up to 2100).

Mail-Boat : During the winter the mail-boat sails each day to Holyhead, and can accommodate a small number of cars. In summer cars are taken only on the car-ferry. The crossing takes $3\frac{1}{2}$ hours.

Fares :

£3.10 1st class; £2.10 2nd class.

Car-Ferry : In summer there are thrice-weekly sailings of the car-ferry to Holyhead (Monday, Tuesday and Saturday).

Fares :
£2.30 (one class)

LIFFEY FERRIES

Crosses between Cardiff Lane and North Wall Quay, and North Wall Quay and Britain Quay Monday to Friday 0730 to 1830. Saturday 0730–2130. Crossings made as often as there are passengers to be carried. Price 3p.

BUSES

The state-owned transport system controlled by Córas Iompair Éireann (C.I.E.) operates a network of over 120 bus-routes in and around the city. Most of the routes connect suburbs at different sides of the city and pass through O'Connell Street in the city centre. An official bus and train timetable is published bi-annually costing 3p and containing a useful map of city bus routes. Do not, however, place too much faith in the scheduled time of departure and arrival, particularly in the rush-hour periods of 0800 to 0900; 1230 to 1430 and 1630 to 1800 where 15-minute delays or more are all too common.

BUS SERVICES

1 City Centre (Parnell Square East)—Ringsend (Pigeon House)
2 City Centre (Parnell Square East)—Westland Row—Ringsend—**Sandymount** (Green)
3 Whitehall—Drumcondra—City Centre (O'Connell Street)—Ringsend—**Sandymount**
4 Annamoe Road—Phibsboro—City Centre (O'Connell Street)—Baggot Street—**Ballsbridge**
5 City Centre (Eden Quay)—Ballsbridge—Mount Merrion Avenue—**Kilmacud**
6 City Centre (Eden Quay)—Ballsbridge—Merrion Road—Blackrock (**Castlebyrne Park**)
6A City Centre (Eden Quay)—Ballsbridge—Merrion Road—Blackrock (**Granville Park**)
7A City Centre (Eden Quay)—Ballsbridge—Blackrock—Dun Laoghaire—**Sallynoggin**
8 City Centre (Eden Quay)—Blackrock—Dun Laoghaire—Sandycove—**Dalkey**
10 Phoenix Park—Phibsboro—City Centre (O'Connell Street)—St Stephen's Green—Donnybrook (**Belfield**)
11 Griffith Avenue—Drumcondra—City Centre (O'Connell Street)—Ranelagh—**Clonskea**
11A Griffith Avenue—Drumcondra—City Centre (O'Connell Street)—Ranelagh—**Foster Avenue**

85

11B City Centre (Parnell Square)—Ranelagh—**Clonskea** (Belfield)
12 Cabra—Phibsboro—City Centre (O'Connell Street)—Ranelagh—**Palmerston Park**
13 Ballymun Road—Glasnevin—Whitworth Road—City Centre (O'Connell Street)—Ranelagh—Beechwood
14 Phoenix Park—Phibsboro—City Centre (O'Connell Street)—Rathmines—Churchtown (Braemor Road)
14A City Centre (D'Olier Street)—Rathmines—**Churchtown** (Meadow Grove)
15A City Centre (D'Olier Street)—Harcourt Street—Rathmines—Rathgar—**Terenure** (Whitehall Road)
15B City Centre (D'Olier Street)—Rathmines—Rathgar—Terenure—**Grange Road**
16 Santry—Drumcondra—City Centre (O'Connell Street)—Harold's Cross—Terenure—**Grange Road**
16A Beaumont—Drumcondra—City Centre (O'Connell Street)—Harold's Cross—Terenure—**Rathfarnham**
17 Dolphin's Barn — Crumlin — Terenure — Churchtown — **Blackrock** (Newtown Avenue)
18 Sandymount (Green)—Ballsbridge—Rathmines—Larkfield Gardens—**Ballyfermot**
19 Cedarwood Road—Ballygall Road East—Phibsboro—City Centre (O'Connell Street)—Dolphin's Barn—Rialto
19A Cedarwood Road—Ballymun Avenue—Phibsboro—City Centre (O'Connell Street)—Dolphin's Barn—Rialto
20 Donnycarney—Fairview—City Centre—St Stephen's Green—Dolphin's Barn—Bulfin Road
20A City Centre (Lower Abbey Street)—Connolly Station—North Strand—Fairview—Donnycarney North
21 City Centre (College Street)—Thomas Street—James Street—Kilmainham—Inchicore (Ring Street)
21A City Centre (College Street)—Thomas Street—James Street—Kilmainham—Inchicore (Bluebell)
22 Cabra West (Ratoath Road) Phibsboro—City Centre (O'Connell Street)—**Dolphin's Barn**—Drimnagh (Mourne Road)
22A Cabra West (Broombridge Road)—Phibsboro—City Centre (O'Connell Street)—Dolphin's Barn—**Drimnagh** (Mourne Road)
23 Jones's Road—Parnell Street—Capel Street—Islandbridge—**Drimnagh** (Galtymore Road)
24 Marino—Fairview—City Centre—North Quay—**Phoenix Park**
25 City Centre (Bachelor's Walk)—Islandbridge—Chapelizod—Palmerstown—Lucan
26 City Centre (Bachelor's Walk)—Islandbridge—Chapelizod—**Palmerstown**
27 City Centre (Eden Quay)—Fairview—Artane—Coolock—**Kilmore**
27A City Centre (Eden Quay)—Fairview—Artane—Kilmore—**Castletimon**
28 City Centre (Lower Abbey Street)—Fairview—Howth Road—Harmonstown Road—Edenmore
29 City Centre (Lower Abbey Street)—Fairview—Howth Road—St Anne's Estate—Raheny
29A City Centre (Lower Abbey Street)—Fairview—Howth Road—St Anne's Estate—Raheny (Newgrove Cross)
30 City Centre (Marlboro Street)—Connolly Station—Fairview—Clontarf—Dollymount
31 City Centre (Lower Abbey Street)—Fairview—Raheny—Sutton Cross—**Howth**
31A City Centre (Lower Abbey Street)—Fairview—Raheny—Sutton Cross—**Strand Road** (Sutton)
32 City Centre (Abbey Street)—Fairview—Raheny—Baldoyle—Portmarnock—Malahide
32B City Centre (Abbey Street)—Fairview—Raheny—**Baldoyle**
33 City Centre (Lower Abbey Street)—Swords—Lusk—Rush—Skerries—**Balbriggan**
34 City Centre (Bachelor's Walk)—Church Street—Glasnevin—**Finglas** (McKelvey Avenue)
34A City Centre (Bachelor's Walk)—Church Street—Glasnevin—**Finglas** (Cr. Kildonan Road)
35 City Centre (Parnell Street)—Whitworth Road—Glasnevin Cemetery—Finglas—(Ballygall Road)
36 City Centre (Parnell Square West)—Drumcondra—Griffith Avenue—**Ballymun Estate** (Sillogue)
36A City Centre (Parnell Square West)—Drumcondra—Griffith Avenue—**Ballymun Estate** (Shangan)
36B City Centre (Parnell Square West)—Drumcondra—Griffith Avenue—**Ballymun Estate** (Santry Avenue)
37 City Centre (Aston Quay)—Northern Quays—Manor Street—Blackhorse Avenue—Villa Park

38 City Centre **(Aston Quay)**—Northern Quays—Manor Street—Navan Road—Kinvara Park

38A City Centre **(Aston Quay)**—Church Street—Phibsboro—Navan Road—Ashtown

39 City Centre **(Aston Quay)**—Manor Street—Navan Road—Castleknock—Blanchardstown

39A City Centre **(Aston Quay)**—Manor Street—Navan Road—Castleknock—Clonsilla

40 City Centre **(Parnell Street)**—Whitworth Road—Glasnevin Cemetery—Finglas (Plunkett Road)

40A City Centre **(Parnell Street)**—Whitworth Road—Glasnevin Cemetery—Finglas (Cappagh Road)

40B City Centre **(Parnell Street)**—Whitworth Road—Glasnevin Cemetery—Finglas (Dubber Cross)

41 City Centre **(Lower Abbey Street)**—Whitehall—Santry—Cloghran—Swords (Glassmore)

41A City Centre (Lower Abbey Street)—Whitehall—Santry—**Dublin Airport**

41B City Centre (Lower Abbey Street)—Whitehall—Santry—Cloghran—Rathbeale—Swords—Rolestown

42 City Centre (Eden Quay)—Coolock—Balgriffin—Kinsealy—**Malahide**

42A City Centre (Eden Quay)—Fairview—Artane—Brookwood Avenue—**Harmonstown**

42B City Centre (Eden Quay)—Fairview—Artane—Gracefield Road—Harmonstown

44 City Centre **(Poolbeg Street)**—Ranelagh—Dundrum—Stepaside—Kilternan—Enniskerry

44A City Centre **(Marlboro Street)**—Fairview—Haddon Road—Castle Avenue—Mount Prospect Avenue

44B City Centre (Poolbeg Street)—Glencullen

45 City Centre **(Poolbeg Street)**—Blackrock—Cabinteely—Shankill—**Bray**

45A Dun Laoghaire—Sallynoggin—Ballybrack—Shankill—Bray

46 City Centre **(College Street)**—Ballsbridge—Mount Merrion—Cabinteely—Shankill

46A City Centre **(College Street)**—Leeson Street—Donnybrook—Mount Merrion—Dun Laoghaire

47 City Centre **(Townsend Street)**—Rathmines—Rathfarnham—Whitechurch—Tibradden—**Rockbrook**

47A City Centre **(Hawkins Street)**—Rathmines—Rathgar—Orwell Road—**Churchtown**

47B City Centre **(Townsend Street)**—Rathmines—Rathfarnham—Ballyboden—Whitechurch—**Grange Road**

48A City Centre **(Poolbeg Street)**—Ranelagh—Milltown—Dundrum—**Ballinteer**

49 City Centre **(Bachelor's Walk)**—Harold's Cross—Terenure—Templeogue—Tallaght

49A City Centre **(Bachelor's Walk)**—Terenure—Templeogue—**Bohernabreena**

50A City Centre **(Fleet Street)**—Patrick Street—Cork Street—Dolphin's Barn—Drimnagh

50 City Centre **(Fleet Street)**—Patrick Street—Cork Street—Dolphin's Barn—Crumlin (Corner Whitehall Road)

50B City Centre **(Fleet Street)**—Cork Street—Dolphin's Barn—Halfway House—Walkinstown Cross

51 City Centre **(Aston Quay)**—Inchicore—Naas Road—Newlands Cross—**Clondalkin**

51A City Centre **(Lower Abbey Street)**—Fairview—Griffith Avenue—Gracepark Road—Beaumont

52 City Centre **(Hawkins Street)**—Bath Avenue—Tritonville Road—Gilford Park—Wilfield Road

53 City Centre **(Marlboro Street)**—Amiens Street—North Strand—Church Road—East Wall

53A City Centre **(Marlboro Street)**—Custom House Quay—**North Wall** (Alexander Road)

54A Killester—Fairview—City Centre (Eden Quay)—Kimmage—**Templeville Road**

54 Killester—Fairview—City Centre (Eden Quay)—Kimmage—**Cherryfield Drive**

55 City Centre **(Fleet Street)**—Harold's Cross—Lower Kimmage Road—Captain's Road—Greenhills

56 City Centre **(Fleet Street)**—Cork Street—Dolphin's Barn—Crumlin Road—Walkinstown Avenue

58 Sallynoggin—Dun Laoghaire—Monkstown Avenue—Casement Park—**Kill O' The Grange**

59 Dun Laoghaire—Albert Road—Sandycove—**Killiney**

60 City Centre **(Lower Abbey Street)**—Drumcondra—Ballymun—Boot Inn—**Leas Cross**

61 City Centre **(Hawkins Street)**—St Stephen's Green—Ranelagh—Milltown—**Churchtown**

62 City Centre (**Hawkins Street**)—Ranelagh—Clonskeagh—Goatstown—**Kilmacud Road**
63 City Centre (**College Street**)—Mount Merrion—Foxrock—Carrickmines—**Glenamuck**
64 City Centre (**College Street**)—Ballsbridge—Donnybrook—Mount Merrion—**Kilmacud Road**
64A City Centre (**College Street**)—Leeson Street—Donnybrook—Mount Merrion—**Kilmacud Road**
65 City Centre (**Bachelor's Walk**)—Crooksling—Blessington—Poulaphouca—Ballymore—Ballykocker—**Donard**
66 City Centre (**Bachelor's Walk**)—Chapelizod—Lucan—Leixlip—**Maynooth**
67 City Centre (**Bachelor's Walk**)—Chapelizod—Palmerstown—Lucan—**Celbridge**
68 City Centre (**Aston Quay**)—Islandbridge—Inchicore—Clondalkin—**Newcastle**
69 City Centre (**Aston Quay**)—Inchicore—Clondalkin—Saggart—**Rathcoole**
70 City Centre (**Aston Quay**)—Ashtown—Castleknock—Blanchardstown—Mulhuddert—**Dunboyne**
72 City Centre (**Bachelor's Walk**)—Northern Quays—Blackhall Place—Manor Street—**Oxmantown Road**
77 City Centre (**Bachelor's Walk**)—Crumlin Road—Walkinstown—Greenhills—**Tallaght**
78 City Centre (**Aston Quay**)—Thomas Street—Kilmainham—Inchicore Road—**Ballyfermot (Spiddal Park)**
78A City Centre (**Aston Quay**)—Thomas Street—Kilmainham—Inchicore Road—**Ballyfermot (Hospital Gate)**
78B City Centre (**Aston Quay**)—Thomas Street—Kilmainham—Inchicore Road—**Ballyfermot (Drumfin Road)**
79 City Centre (**Aston Quay**)—Northern Quays—Heuston Bridge—St John's Road—**Ballyfermot**
80 City Centre (**Aston Quay**)—Blackhall Place—Ashtown—Castleknock—Luttrellstown—**Clonsilla**
81 City Centre (**Fleet Street**)—Clanbrassil Street—S.C. Road—Clogher Road—Bangor Road (**The Circle**)
83 City Centre (**Fleet Street**)—Sth. Gt. George's Street—Rathmines—Kenilworth Park—**Kimmage**
84 City Centre (**College Street**)—Stillorgan—Bray—Greystones—Delgany—Kilcoole—**Newcastle**
84A Bray (**Railway Station**)—**Greystones**
85 Bray (**Railway Station**)—Kilcroney—**Enniskerry**
86 City Centre (**College Street**)—Carrickmines—Cabinteely (**Johnstown Park**)
88 Sutton Station—Howth Summit—**Howth**

Fare Concessions

Bus fares, though lower than in London, are by no means cheap, and the minimum adult bus fare of 4p for 1–3 fare stages is especially bad value. Since fares are likely to increase each year, it is good to know of the various concessions available. Children under three years of age who do not occupy a seat to the exclusion of another passenger and are accompanied by a fare-paying passenger may travel free of charge. Children under 16 years of age are charged fares at half the adult rate. There are special reduced rates for school children under 16 years of age, when travelling to and from school up to 1700 Mondays to Fridays and up to 1330 on Saturdays. And for school children who do not relish the thought of school meals, between 1200 and 1400 Monday to Friday there is a charge of only 1p for up to 10 fare stages and 2p for more than 10 stages. For cross-town shopping expeditions there is a reduced charge of 3p for adults and 2p for children, between the hours of 1000 and 1200 midday and 1430 and 1630. Details of these shopping routes are given in the official timetable. Reduced weekly tickets are also issued for 5- or 6-day periods, available for one trip in each direction between two stated points, where the normal single adult fare is at least 10p. The saving on a 10p adult fare for a 5-day period works out at about 15 per cent. Weekly tickets may be purchased at the C.I.E. Administration Office, 59 Upper O'Connell Street, Dublin 1, tel. 46301, or at Busarus, Store Street, tel. 42941. Children under 16 may purchase weekly tickets at half the adult rate.

Passenger Regulations

The enforcement of many of the passenger regulations is left to the discretion of the bus conductors, who are usually very understanding. But since ignorance is no defence in the eyes of the law, it might be useful to be familiar with some of the more relevant regulations. For example : did you know that only 5 passengers are allowed to stand in a bus (none upstairs) and then only at peak periods? Or that you have no right to bring your pet poodle or cheetah or whatever on to the bus without the conductor's permission, and that he can change his mind anytime he likes? Or that you are only allowed 28lbs weight of personal luggage, and that luggage in excess of 28lbs can be charged for at the rate of 4p per article? And you may only bring bulky luggage on to the bus if you have permission from the conductor? And needless to say, whether you pay for your luggage or not, C.I.E. will not be responsible for any loss or damage caused to it. Lastly, you are legally obliged to hand up to the conductor any articles of lost property found on the bus. If you are unfortunate enough to be on the losing end, you may collect lost property at the **Lost Property Office,** 33 Bachelor's Walk, tel. 46301, open from 0900 to 1800 Monday to Friday, 0900 to 1400 on Saturdays.

C.I.E. Information : tel. 47911, weekdays 0900 to 2100, Sundays 1000 to 2100.

TAXIS

There are about 1,400 registered taxis operating in Dublin, too many according to the taxi drivers, but too few as you will undoubtedly discover if you are looking for one on a rainy night. There are a number of small private firms, and three main radio cab groups, operating a 24-hour service, and they can be flagged down on the street or called by telephone. The taximeter indicates the fare to be paid, and this is based on a combination of distance travelled, number of passengers and the time spent. The minimum fare for one is 20p, each additional passenger costs 4p, each article of luggage, 4p, each $\frac{1}{4}$ mile or period of time not exceeding 3 minutes costs 3p. Most taxi drivers expect a tip (and why not?). Meters only operate within a 10 mile radius of the city centre, so for longer journeys the fare should be negotiated in advance. The main radio taxi cabs are :

Blue Cabs, tel 61111, **Co-Op Cabs,** tel. 66666, **Ryans,** tel. 772222

Taxi Ranks and Shelters
Amiens Street, Dublin 1 (near station)

	0800-midnight	43288
Angle, Ranelagh, Dublin 6	Continuous	972735
Aston's Quay, Dublin 2	,,	778053
Burgh Quay, Dublin 2	,,	778191
Cabra Road, Ratoath Road junction	,,	44068
College Green, Dublin 2	,,	777440
Crescent, Malahide Road, Dublin 3	,,	336507
Dún Laoghaire, Co. Dublin	,,	805263
Eccles Street, Dublin 7	,,	778870
Eden Quay, Dublin 1	,,	777054
Harcourt Street, Dublin 2	,,	754693

Lansdowne Road, Dublin 4	Continuous	684222
O'Connell Street Upper, Dublin 1	,,	44599
O'Connell Street Lower, Dublin 1	,,	44491
Rathmines Road Upper, Dublin 6	,,	973276
St John's Road, Dublin	0800–2100	779121
St Stephen's Green North, Dublin 2	Continuous	67381
Westland Row, Dublin 2	,,	773001
Westmoreland Street, Dublin 2	,,	778914

CAR HIRE

Despite the competitiveness of the business—there are over seventy car hire firms in Dublin alone—you will pay appreciably higher rates than in Britain or the U.S. It is difficult to give accurate prices since the charge varies according to the company involved, as well as the time of year, the type of car, and the type of hiring arrangement. Paradoxically, you will find that it is often the larger firms which charge the higher rates, though they do have a more extensive network of offices throughout the country, and can arrange collection and delivery in a wider variety of locations. Most firms will organise delivery and collection at Dublin, Cork and Shannon airports. Both limited and unlimited mileage arrangements are available; for the former there is a lower basic rate, but an additional 2p to 6p is charged per mile.

The type of car to be hired has an important effect on the price : where a Volkswagen may cost £4.00 per day, a Mercedes automatic will cost about £8.00. The other main variable is time of year, resulting in a price difference of approximately 40 to 50 per cent. The 'low' or 'off', or winter season rate is usually from 1 October to 1 May, though some firms have special economy rates for May and June, the interim period between the low and high season. To give some guidance in the matter of cost, a Volkswagen from a middle-priced firm will cost about £15.00 a week for unlimited mileage in the off season, and about £24.00 weekly during the summer.

Hirers must produce a current unendorsed driving licence of their own country, or an international driving licence, valid in Ireland. An Irish licence will not usually be accepted from a hirer normally resident outside Ireland. The age requirement is usually between 21 years and 65 years; some companies demand a minimum requirement of 26 years, and may insist on special insurance provisions for those younger than 26, or older than 65. Third party insurance is mandatory, and usually included in the hire charge; full insurance cover can be arranged at about 60p per day.

SOME DUBLIN CAR-HIRE FIRMS

ABC Rent-A-Car, 179 Pearse Street, Dublin 2. Tel. 773948/774703. Night: 350713

Auto Drive Ltd, 9/10 Arran Quay, Dublin 2. Tel. 770576. Night: 889345

Avis Rent-A-Car, 1 Hanover Street, Dublin 7. Tel. 776971. Also at Dublin Airport. Tel. 376304

Bolands Car Rentals, 179 Pearse Street, Dublin 2. Tel. 43186

Budget Rent-A-Car, 176 Pembroke Road. Tel. 685064

Dennis Car Rentals, 48 New Street, Dublin 8. Tel. 780033

Economy Car Hire, 24 Lower Abbey Street, Dublin 1. Tel. 40109

Kenning Car Hire (Ireland), 42 Westland Row, Dublin 2. Tel. 772723 (Offices in England, Scotland and France)

Murray Rent-A-Car, Baggot Street Bridge, Dublin 2. Tel. 63221; also Dublin Airport, tel. 378179 and 24 Upper O'Connell Street, Dublin 1. Tel. 43937

Ryans/Hertz Car Hire, 17/22 Pearse Street. Tel. 772971 and Dublin Airport. Tel. 371693

Dan Ryan Rent-A-Car, 42 Parkgate Street, Dublin 8. Tel. 779117 and Dublin Airport. Tel. 372412

Shelbourne Car Hire, 2 Haddington Road, Dublin 4. Tel. 60805. Night: 974373

Waldens Self-Drive, 172 Parnell Street, Dublin 1. Tel. 47831 (probably the cheapest rates available)

SELF-DRIVE MINI-BUS HIRE

Hire charges range from £35.00 to £50.00 per week.
Among the companies with coaches for hire are :

Enzo Coaches, 12 Carysfort Avenue, Blackrock. Tel.
886930

Lavery & Sons, 76 Stannoway Road, Dublin 12. Tel.
977944 (24-hour service)

Maloney, Fingal Service Station, Airport Road, Dublin 9.
Tel. 310841

Purcell Car Hire, Linders Garage Ltd, 30 Arran Quay,
Dublin 2. Tel. 776661

Shelbourne Car Hire (See above)

DORMOBILE HIRE

Hire charges are between £40.00 and £50.00 per week.

Irish Car Rentals, 57B Harcourt Street, Dublin 2. Tel.
752145

Johnson & Perrot, 12 South Leinster Street, Dublin 2. Tel.
67213

Maloney (See above)

HIRE A COACH AND DRIVER

Silverdale Travel, Parliament Street, Dublin 2. Tel. 751830,
757168

Coachways Ltd, 10 Grafton Arcade, Dublin 2. Tel. 779829

PAB, 19 Parliament Street, Dublin 2. Tel. 773293

M. R. Dorgan, 36 Wasdale Park, Dublin 6. Tel. 909569

ALL-NIGHT PETROL STATIONS
(GAS STATIONS)

Autocars, Milltown Road, Dublin 6. Tel. 975156

Belmont Service Station, 126 Sandford Road, Dublin 6.
Tel. 978204

Jet Filling Station, 147 Townsend Street, Dublin 2. Tel.
778740

C.S.E. Garage, North Frederick Street, Dublin 1. Tel.
46511

P. R. Reilly, Howth Road, Killester. Tel. 336924
Ryan's, 19/20 Pearse Street, Dublin 2. Tel. 772971
Smiths, Merrion Road. Tel. 693911

ALL-NIGHT BREAKDOWN SERVICE

Mr. Reilly, Central Towing Service, 41 Foley Street. **Tel.**
47580
Mr. Merriott, 55 Clonskeagh Road. Tel. 979537
Motor & Machines, Main Street, Dundrum, Dublin 14.
Tel. 983911

MOTORING ORGANISATIONS

Automobile Association (AA), 23 Suffolk Street, Dublin 2.
Tel. 779481
Royal Irish Automobile Club (RIAC), 34 Dawson Street,
Dublin 2. Tel. 775141
Motor Registration Office (for visitor's licence), Coleraine
Street. Tel. 49981

MILEAGES FROM DUBLIN

Armagh **80**	Killarney **191**
Athlone **78**	Limerick **123**
Belfast **103**	Rosslare Harbour **98**
Cork **161**	Sligo **135**
Derry **145**	Tipperary **112**
Donegal **150**	Tralee **187**
Drogheda **30**	Waterford **103**
Dundalk **52**	Wexford **86**
Galway **133**	Wicklow **31**
Kilkenny **73**	

SPORT & RECREATION

BADMINTON

Irish Badminton Association, Badminton Hall, Whitehall Road, Terenure, Dublin 6. Tel. 505966

BALLOONING

Contact David Synott of the **Ballooning Association of Ireland,** 50 Mountjoy Square, Dublin 1. Tel. 41497

BALLROOM DANCING

The **Society of Amateur Ballroom Dancing** is contacted through the Hon. Secretary, 80 Leinster Avenue, Dublin 3

OLD-TIME DANCING

Enquiries to the Secretary, **National Association of Old Time Dancers,** 53 Kincora Avenue, Clontarf. Tel. 337742

BOWLING (Outdoor)

Contact the **Bowling League of Ireland,** 14 Brian Road, Marino, Dublin 3, tel. 338148. There are bowling greens at Herbert Park, Ballsbridge, tel. 684364, where play is free. Also at Clontarf Golf Club, Dublin 3, tel. 332669; Willie Pearse Memorial Park, Crumlin, tel. 502782; Moran Park, Dun Laoghaire, tel 804044. Flat soled shoes are a must!

BOWLING (Ten-pin)

Stillorgan Bowl, Stillorgan, Co. Dublin. Tel. 881656/7. Open from 1000. Reduced rates up to 1800 Monday to Friday. There are 24 lanes; free instruction; snack bar, car-park. It is reached by the 46, 46A, 63, 84, 86 buses.

CHESS

The **Dublin Chess Club,** at 20 Lincoln Place, Dublin, provides chess facilities from 1900 to 2330 every Monday and Thursday. If you require a drink for inspiration, the **Pembroke Bar,** Pembroke Street, has chess sets available for customers.

CINEMA

The **Irish Film Society** have a number of film seasons each year and organise discussions, lectures and amateur film-making. For details contact The Secretary, 12 Merrion Square, Dublin 2. Tel. 866213. The **Dublin Cine Club,** 65 Harcourt Street, also provides lectures, films and discussions.

DOG-BREEDING

Meetings and dog shows are organised by the **Irish Kennel Club,** 4 Harcourt Street, Dublin 2. Tel. 758126

DRAMA

There are hundreds of amateur drama societies throughout the country and many in Dublin. For details of one in your area, contact The Secretary, **Dublin Area Amateur Drama League,** 24 Carragh Road, Dublin.

FENCING

You can contact the **Irish Amateur Fencing Association,** c/o Royal Bank of Ireland, Lansdowne Road, Dublin 4, tel. 885081, or the only school of fencing in Ireland—**Salle Duffy,** Salle d'Armes, St John's Road, Sandymount, Dublin 4, tel. 693720. Beginners' lessons are given on Tuesdays at 1900. Visitors to Dublin are welcome, and may avail of temporary membership. Equipment may be purchased or hired.

FISHING

SEA ANGLING There is good sea fishing in **Dublin Bay,** including mackerel, mullet, whiting, sea-trout, bass, etc. At **Poolbeg lighthouse** bass and sometimes tope are taken. Bass can also be found at **Dollymount** and **Williamstown.** At the rear of **Dún Laoghaire's west pier,** flounders, gurnard and sea trout can be caught. Boats can be hired from **Bullock** and **Coliemore Harbour,** Dalkey, and medium sized pollock, codfish and mackerel can be caught off Dalkey sound in the summer, and whiting in **Killiney Bay** in winter. Boats can also be hired at **Dún Laoghaire pier** and at **Howth** where pollock and mackerel can be fished off **Ireland's Eye.**

FRESH-WATER There is good salmon and trout fishing in the Liffey, particularly from February to May, but most of it is preserved. There is also good brown trout fishing between **Celbridge** and **Clane,** and the **Dublin Trout Anglers Association,** c/o Major P. McDonagh, 151 Fortfield Park, Dublin 5, exercises fishing rights over much of the area. **Poulaphouca** and **Leixlip Lake** reservoir have brown trout, and permits may be purchased from fishing tackle shops in Dublin. The **river Dodder,** which suffers from increasing pollution problems, has small- and medium-sized trout, and the **Bohernabreena Reservoir** has trout fly fishing. Permits are obtained from the City Manager, Town Clerk, 28 Castle Street, for these and for the Roundwood Reservoir. The **Broadmeadows river,** near Swords has brown trout and sea trout, but visitors must be accompanied by members of the Swords Angling Club (contact The Secretary, R. Shortt, Church Road, Swords, Co. Dublin).

LICENCES A licence for all 17 fishing districts in Ireland for a full season costs £4.00. For a specific district the charge is £3.00, and a licence lasting 21 days for all areas is also £3.00; and for 7 days is £1.00. Licences are available from fishing tackle shops, and the Clerk of the Dublin Board of Conservators, 58 Dame Street, Dublin 2, tel. 774456. Among the main tackle shops are **Garnetts and Keegan,** 31 Parliament Street, Dublin 2, tel. 777472; **Moorkens** Ltd., Upper Abbey Street, Dublin 1, tel. 45704, and **Rory's Fishing Tackle,** 17a Temple Bar, Dublin 1, tel. 772351.

FLYING

Leinster Aero Club, Dublin Airport, tel. 376473 and 379900, ext 265. **Irish Aero Club,** Cloghran, Co. Dublin, tel. 378323, 355228, or 379900 ext. 699. This club has 4 full-time instructors, 5 Cessna 150s, 2 Cessna 172s, a Cessna 310 and an Anster JIN. There are club facilities, a bar and courses for the P.P.L., C.P.L., night rating, instrument rating, multi-engine rating and aerobatics.

GAELIC FOOTBALL

It has the largest spectator following of any sport in Ireland. The All-Ireland Championship (inter-county) finals are played on the fourth Sunday of September at Croke Park; for details of matches and local clubs contact **G.A.A., Croke Park,** Jones's Road, Dublin 7. Tel. 48607

GLIDING

Instruction and facilities available on a day-membership basis of 50p or annual membership of £15.00, with the **Dublin Gliding Club,** Flat 15, Glendale Court, Adelaide Street, Dún Laoghaire.

GOLF

There are 27 golf clubs within a 20-mile radius of the city, 16 of them full 18-hole courses. There is a long waiting-list for membership of most clubs; however visitors are welcomed during the week though they may have difficulty playing at weekends and bank holidays. Green fees vary from 25p to £1.00 for a visitor playing with a member, and 75p to £2.00 for a visitor alone. Many of the clubs have a special weekly rate. It is advisable to telephone the club secretary in advance to enquire about fees and facilities. The courses listed below are 18-hole, unless specified.

Within 6 miles :

The Castle Golf Club, Rathfarnham	Tel. 905835
Clontarf Golf Club, Clontarf	Tel. 332669

Edmonstown, Rathfarnham	Tel. 907461
Elm Park, Donnybrook	Tel. 693438
Grange, Rathfarnham	Tel. 905832
Foxrock Golf Club, Foxrock (9-hole)	Tel. 895668
Milltown Golf Club	Tel. 977060
Newlands Golf Club, Clondalkin	Tel. 592903
Rathfarnham Golf Club, Rathfarnham	Tel. 905201
St Anne's, Dollymount (9-hole)	Tel. 332797
Royal Dublin, Dollymount	Tel. 337153

Within 12 miles:

Carrickmines Golf Club, Co. Dublin (9-hole)	Tel. 895676
Dun Laoghaire Golf Club, Co. Dublin	Tel. 803916
Howth Golf Club, Howth	Tel. 323055
Hermitage Golf Club, Lucan, Co. Dublin	Tel. 364549
The Island Golf Club, Malahide, Co. Dublin	Tel. 350595
Killiney Golf Club, Killiney (9-hole)	Tel. 851983
Malahide Golf Club, Malahide (9-hole)	Tel. 350248
Lucan Golf Club, Lucan, Co. Dublin (9-hole)	Tel. 280248
Portmarnock Golf Club, Co. Dublin	Tel. 323082
Sutton Golf Club, Sutton, Co. Dublin (9-hole)	Tel. 323013
Woodbrook Golf Club, Bray	Tel. 862073

Within 20 miles:

Rush Golf Club, Rush, Co. Dublin (9-hole)	Tel. 207548
Skerries Golf Club, Co. Dublin (9-hole)	Tel. 291204
Donabate Golf Club, Co. Dublin	Tel. 350335
Bray Golf Club, Co. Wicklow (9-hole)	Tel. 862092
Balbriggan Golf Club, Co. Dublin (9-hole)	Tel. 212173

GOLF DRIVING RANGES:

John Jacobs School, Leopardstown Race Course	Tel. 895341
Elm Park Golf Course, Donnybrook	Tel. 893361
Clare Manor Hotel, Malahide Road, Coolock	Tel. 311604
Spawell Golf Range, Tallaght, Co. Dublin	Tel. 907990

GREYHOUND RACING

Shelbourne Park, Dublin 4, tel. 683502, on Mondays, Wednesdays and Saturdays at 2000. Buses 2 and 3.

Harold's Cross Stadium, Dublin 6, tel.971081, on Tuesdays, Thursdays and Fridays at 2000. Buses 16, 54 and 55. The season is from February to early December; admission is from 10p to 30p and both tracks have bars, restaurants, tote (parimutuel) and book-makers.

HORSE-RIDING

The average cost for one hour's hacking is 75p; riding instruction costs about £1.00 an hour, half-day treks from £1.50 and full-day treks about £2.50. Below are a selection of the riding stables in and around Dublin.

Burton Hall Riding Establishment,
Foxrock, Co. Dublin   Tel. 893204

Miss Iris P. Kellett, 39 Mespil Road, Dublin 4   Tel. 61216

Magee's Riding Stables,
Castleknock, Co. Dublin   Tel. 383458

Malahide Riding School,
Grand Hotel, Malahide, Co. Dublin   Tel. 350987

R. K. MacDodd,
Phœnix Park, Castleknock, Co. Dublin   Tel. 383319

Sean Finlay,
Phœnix Park, Castleknock, Co. Dublin   Tel. 383567

Houlihan's Riding Stables,
North Road, Finglas, Dublin 11   Tel. 342547

HORSE RACING

There are 7 race courses within a 30-mile radius of the city centre, three of them within 8 miles, and they provide over 80 afternoon and evening meetings during the year. **Phœnix Park Race Course** is 3 miles, **Leopardstown** 6 miles, and **Baldoyle** 8 miles from the city centre. **The Curragh,** twenty miles from Dublin, stages the prestigious Irish Sweeps Derby and other classics. **Fairyhouse** in Co. Meath is 17 miles, **Naas** 18 miles, and **Punchestown** which has an important 3-day meeting in April is 30 miles from the city. There are special buses and trains operated by C.I.E. for most race meetings.

Fixtures List (E=evening meeting)

January 1 Baldoyle; **8** Naas; **15** Leopardstown; **29** Naas.

February 2 Fairyhouse; **5** Leopardstown; **12** Punchestown; **19** Leopardstown; **26** Baldoyle.

March 4 Naas; **17** Baldoyle; **18** Naas; **22** Leopardstown; **25** Phœnix Park.

April 1 Phœnix Park; **3** Fairyhouse; **4** Fairyhouse; **5** Fairyhouse; **8** Curragh; **15** Naas; **22** Curragh; **25** Punchestown; **26** Punchestown; **27** Punchestown; **29** Phœnix Park.

May 3 Phœnix Park (E); **6** Leopardstown; **8** Leopardstown (E); **13** Curragh; **17** Curragh; **27** Phœnix Park; **31** Leopardstown (E).

June 1 Naas (E); **3** Naas; **5** Baldoyle; **10** Leopardstown; **14** Curragh (E); **17** Baldoyle; **21** Phœnix Park.

July 1 Curragh; **5** Baldoyle (E); **8** Phœnix Park; **11** Curragh (E); **15** Leopardstown; **22** Curragh; **26** Baldoyle (E); **28** Phœnix Park (E); **29** Phœnix Park.

August 5 Leopardstown; **9** Phœnix Park (E); **12** Phœnix Park; **19** Curragh; **23** Leopardstown; **26** Baldoyle.

September 2 Curragh; **9** Phœnix Park; **13** Curragh; **16** Curragh; **23** Curragh; **30** Leopardstown.

October 7 Phœnix Park; **11** Punchestown; **14** Naas; **21** Curragh; **25** Fairyhouse; **26** Leopardstown.

November 2 Punchestown; **4** Curragh; **8** Fairyhouse; **11** Naas; **18** Leopardstown; **22** Baldoyle.

December 2 Naas; **6** Leopardstown; **9** Fairyhouse; **16** Punchestown; **26** Leopardstown; **27** Leopardstown; **30** Punchestown.

HURLING

One of the fastest ball games in the world; the All-Ireland finals are played at Croke Park, Dublin, on the first Sunday in September. For details contact **G.A.A., Croke Park, Jones's Road, Dublin 7.** Tel. 48607

JUDO

Dublin Judo Club, 32 Parkgate Street, Dublin 7. Tel. 775782

KARTING

Contact **Mr Trevor Williams,** 64 Park Avenue, Ballsbridge, Dublin 4

LIFE-SAVING

If you want to learn how to save yourself or others, contact the **Royal Life Saving Society,** 209 Clonliffe Road, Dublin 3. The **Irish Red Cross,** 16 Merrion Square, Dublin 2, tel. 65135, also instructs in water safety and rescue.

MOUNTAINEERING

Associate membership is available to anyone over 17 years of age, with the **Irish Mountaineering Club.** Courses are given in Dalkey Quarry and Glendalough in summer, and lectures in the winter. Contact the Secretary, Irish Mountaineering Club, 6 Lennox Street, South Circular Road, Dublin 8

PHOTOGRAPHY

Contact the **Dublin Camera Club,** 60 Lower Baggot Street, Dublin 2

POLO

Polo is played in the **Phœnix Park** three times a week, on Tuesdays, Thursdays and Sundays, from the end of April to the beginning of September. Games usually begin at 1530 and admission is free (the only free polo grounds in the world) to spectators and players.

SHOOTING AND GAME

Under the Game Birds Protection order made by the Department of Lands, the following birds may be shot in season :

Grouse : 12 August to 30 September (except in Cork, Kerry, Mayo—1 to 30 September)

Mallard, wigeon, teal, pintail and **white fronted geese :** 1 September to 31 January

Partridge : 1 November to 15 November

Cock Pheasant : 1 November to 31 January

Hares : 26 September to 28 February

It is strictly **prohibited** to kill or take **green plover** (lapwing), **hen pheasant, brent geese, barnacle geese, greylag geese, quail** and **landrail** (corncrake) or kill and take **hares** except by coursing or beagling under permit in counties where hare protection orders are in force.

Even more strictly enforced, particularly since the Northern crisis, are regulations concerning the **licensing of firearms.** Firearms certificates are necessary, and must be renewed each year. Certificates valid outside the State are not acceptable. The fees for certificates for shotguns are £3.25 for the first gun and 75p for each additional gun, and £1.50 for each rifle. Applications for certificates must be sent to the Secretary, Department of Justice, Upper Merrion Street, Dublin 2. Double-barrel guns only are allowed; if repeater guns are carried only two cartridges must be loaded; all guns must carry third party insurance. For information on shooting areas contact : **Dublin Regional Game Council,** Bothar na Breena, Tallaght, Co. Dublin, the organisation's secretary, Mr. M. J. Downes, tel. 505118, or Garnett and Keegan (Gunsmiths) of Parliament Street.

SKIING

The **Ski Club of Ireland,** Knockrabo Sports Centre, Mount
Anville Road, Goatstown, tel. 693985 (984149 after 1900)
and the **Irish Ski School** at Santry Stadium (enquiries to
84 Old Kilmainham, Dublin 8, tel. 754483) organise skiing
holidays, and lessons and practice sessions on dry-slopes.

SWIMMING

Despite the increase in pollution, it is still safe to swim
in the open sea at Dollymount Strand, the Bull Wall,
Sutton, Howth, Portmarnock, and Malahide, all within
9 miles of the city centre on the north side, and at Sandymount, Sandycove, Seapoint, Dún Laoghaire and Dalkey,
all within 10 miles of the centre on the south side.
Nevertheless, for a city with such a fast expanding
population, the number of public swimming pools available is chronically inadequate. Also, for some inexplicable
reason, most of them are open for a shorter period on
Sundays, which one would presume to be the most popular
day. However they are inexpensive. There are a number of
private pools which occasionally allow the public to use
their facilities at such ungodly hours as 08.00 one morning
each week. You have to join or form a special swimming
club, and admission is more difficult than for the most
exclusive dining clubs. At the time of writing the Forty
Foot in Sandycove, Dublin's traditional men-only bathing
spot is still men only—but for how long?

PUBLIC SWIMMING BATHS

Clontarf : Open sea bathing May to September. Monday
to Friday 1000 to 2100, Saturday 1000 to 1800. Sunday
1000 to 1300, 1400 to 1800.

Markievicz Baths, Townsend Street : Monday to Friday
1000 to 2100. Saturday 1000 to 1800. Sunday 1000 to
1400. Admission 13p for adults, 6p for children.

Willie Pearse Pool, Windmill Street, Dublin 12 : Monday
to Friday 1400 to 1600 and 2000 to 2300 in winter.

From June to September, 1000 to 1800 and 2000 to 2300. Saturday 1000 to 1300 and 1400 to 1800. Sunday 1000 to 1400. Admission 13p for adults, 6p for children.

Blackrock Baths: Open from end of May to end of September. Monday to Saturday 0900 to 2030. Sunday 1000 to 1800. Admission 5p for adults, children and spectators 3p.

Northside Swimming Pool, Coolock: Monday to Friday 1400 to 1600 and 2000 to 2300 in winter. From June to September, 1000 to 1800 and 2000 to 2300. Saturday 1000 to 1300, 1400 to 2000. Sunday 1000 to 1400. Admission 13p for adults, 6p for children.

Dún Laoghaire: Open from end of May to end of September. Monday to Saturday 0900 to 2000. Sunday 1000 to 1800. Admission 5p for adults, 3p for children and spectators. Hot seaweed baths at 17p and Russian steam baths at 25p are available from Monday to Saturday, 1000 to 1800.

TENNIS

There are public courts at **Herbert Park,** Ballsbridge, tel. 684364; **Bushy Park,** Terenure, Dublin 6, tel. 900320; **Ellenfield Park,** Whitehall, Dublin 9, tel. 375538; **St Anne's Estate,** Dollymount, Dublin 3, tel. 332797. The cost is 7p for adults, 3p for children per hour. Rackets cannot be hired.

The **Fitzwilliam Tournament** in July follows Wimbledon in the international tennis circuit.

WATER-SKIING

There are two clubs in Malahide, Co Dublin. The **Penguin Water Ski Club,** Broadmeadows, Malahide, has skiing every Saturday and Sunday at 1500 and on Wednesdays at 1900 from May to September. Day membership is 33p, annual membership £6.30, or £3.15 if you are under 18. They also have an annual family membership at £8.40 and a social membership at £2.10. The ski-tow fee is 30p for the first run, and 20p for subsequent runs. Apply to Miss Rita Ryan, 18 O'Neachtain Road, Drumcondra, tel. 377098. The other club, which has boats for hire, and a lower membership fee, is the **Dublin Balscadden Power and Ski Club,** The Strand, Malahide. Membership is £7.00 for men, £5.00 for ladies and £9.00 for a family membership.

YOUNG PEOPLE IN DUBLIN

INFANTS AND MOTHERS

THE recent increase in day and night nurseries is presumably not unconnected with the rise of Women's Lib, and a good thing too. However, as far as babysitting is concerned, there is no substitute for the neighbour's teenage daughter, if you can afford her telephone bills. I hesitate to recommend or influence a decision as important as choosing a day nursery, children's crèche or babysitting service, but on the understanding that you check the service, personally or through a friend, I mention a few. The **Haddington Road Nursery,** 38 Haddington Road, Dublin 4, tel. 67871, operates an overnight service. The charge per child is about £1.00. The **Teddy Crèche,** 31 Lavarna Grove, Terenure, tel. 903883, charges £2.25 per night, £1.50 per day and £1.00 per half day. The most professional service is offered by **Childminders,** 22 Kildare Street, tel. 67981. They supply babysitters to your home at 30p an hour, and transportation to and from your home is their responsibility, not yours. They also supply temporary 'house mothers' who will look after the children and run the house. The charge is £16.00 a week, or £2.50 per day. Most of the A* and A grade hotels run an infant or babysitting service for residents. The **Civics Institute of Ireland,** 20 North Frederick Street, Dublin 1, tel. 46911, manage ten **Children's Play Centres** for Dublin Corporation, providing art, dancing, games and physical education. They have two Day Nursery Centres, for the 2–5 year olds age group of children; the nurseries, **St Brigid's,** Mountjoy Square, and **St Joseph's,** Maryland, Cork Street, Dublin 8, are open from 0830 to 1800 5 days a week. **St Brigid's Day Nursery,** Henrietta Street, looks after the children of mothers who have to work; payment depends on circumstances.

If you want to hire baby's suncars, cots, mattresses, try **Sheeran's Baby Carriage Service,** 70 Talbot Street, Dublin 1, tel. 419531, or **Mrs. D. Nolan,** 13 Woodbine Park, Blackrock, Co. Dublin, tel. 691803. She charges £1.00 a week for the hire of a cot and mattress, 75p for a go-car, with a 35p collection or delivery charge. Incredibly, she operates a 7-day, 24-hour service, at no extra cost.

The **Dublin Health Authority,** Carnegie Centre, 21/25 Lord Edward Street, Dublin 2, tel. 776811, offers Child Health Services to all children up to 6 years of age; free medical examination, advice and guidance is given. Other useful addresses :

The National Children's Hospital, Harcourt Street, tel. 754069/752355. The social service and psychiatric unit offers a preventive as well as therapeutic service.

The Children's Hospital, Social Science Department, Temple Street, Dublin 1. Tel. 48763.

Our Lady's Hospital for Sick Children, Crumlin, Dublin 12. Tel. 503111/506966.

Fertility Guidance Clinic, 10 Merrion Square, Dublin 2. Tel. 63676. Non-denominational family planning service and advice on infertility and marital problems.

CHILDREN AND TEENAGERS

Children are reasonably well catered for in Dublin but it is mainly on an informal basis. There are, for example, no children's museums or cinemas, few hotels or restaurants provide specific children's menus, and you can expect even fewer to give children the proverbial Italian-style welcome in their establishments.

Whatever their age most children prefer to choose their own way of spending their day, but if you are on holiday in Dublin or are a parent exhausted after the first month of the summer holiday and dreading the other two months to come, you might respectfully suggest to your offspring some of the following diversions :

PUBLIC PARKS Apart from the obvious ones such as **Phœnix Park** and **St Stephen's Green**, which is open from 0800 weekdays and 1000 Sundays until dusk, there are among others **Palmerston Park, Fairview Park, St Patrick's Park, Bushy Park** in Terenure and perhaps the most under-utilised of them all, **Herbert Park**, Ballsbridge.

PHŒNIX PARK does of course offer the most possibilities. Covering 1760 acres it is one of the finest enclosed parks in the world and can be reached by a short bus journey on the Nos. 10, 14, 23, 24 or 25. There are three riding stables, a race course, polo grounds (admission free to the thrice-weekly games on Tuesdays, Thursdays and Sundays), and, of course, miles of playing fields and recreation areas. Remember however that the park is extensively used by learner-drivers, so walk, cycle or drive with that in mind. Open from 0830 Monday to Friday, from 1030 Saturdays and 1000 Sundays; closing time varies according to the time of sunset, from around 1600 in December and January to 2130 in June and July. Check details with the Superintendent, tel. 383021.

THE ZOOLOGICAL GARDENS Founded in 1830, the Dublin Zoo, situated within Phœnix Park, is the third oldest zoo in the world. Although included in the children's section here, it provides interest and facilities for all ages. The Zoo has an international reputation for lion-breeding, is noted for its Reticulated Giraffes and Gibbon Monkeys and has the usual complement of tigers, elephants, bears, seals, reptiles and unhappy baboons. There is a Pets Corner for children which costs an extra $2\frac{1}{2}$p, pony rides also

$2\frac{1}{2}$p and miniature train ride, 5p. Push chairs can be hired at the entrance for 15p. There is a good restaurant, one of the few in Dublin with special portions for children at reduced prices. The Zoo is open from 0930 (1200 on Sundays) to 1800 in summer and till dusk in the winter months. Admission : 30p for adults, 15p for children under 14. Children under 3 are free. For further details tel. 771426.

SPORT Most of the sporting activities are outlined in the **Sports** section but a little information on sports instruction may be of use. Most swimming pools run **swimming lessons** for children, costing a couple of pounds per course.

Lessons are given free at **Clontarf** every morning in the summer. On Saturdays, between 1000 and 1200, the **Irish Handball Association** gives free coaching lessons in Croke Park for boys and girls. Children can learn to **fence**, in **Salle d'Armes**, St John's Road, Sandymount, tel. 693720. Children under 18 can play **tennis** on public courts for 3p an hour. Bring your own rackets (*see* **Tennis**). A number of tennis clubs give coaching to children, including **Sutton Lawn Tennis Club**, **Glasnevin Lawn Tennis Club**, and **Templeogue Lawn Tennis Club**. At Dún Laoghaire, at the **Dublin Yacht Club** moorings, there are **sailing lessons** for children. Life jackets are provided and the charge is 60p for 3 children. Tel. Donald Archibald, 978415. For **Camogie** devotees, **Club na Gael** meets at 5 North George's Street on Thursdays, at 1900 and they organise games and coaching for young players.

HISTORICAL INTEREST Depending on their ages, children may prefer to visit buildings, *see* **Places of Interest.** For example **Christchurch Cathedral,** Lord Edward Street, where the tomb of Strongbow—an effigy of a recumbent warrior with a child lying beside him, supposedly commemorating the story of how Strongbow killed his own son for cowardice in battle—may provide a cautionary tale for erring children. Most children take a macabre delight in shaking hands with the preserved remains of an eight-foot tall crusader, in the vaults of **St Michan's Church** in Church Street. Admission to the vaults, which are only open on Sundays, is 10p for adults, and 5p for children. The **Bank of Ireland,** College Green, formerly the old Parliament House, is steeped in history, and any of the attendants will give visitors a guided tour, free of charge, during normal banking hours. Another place to visit is **Kilmainham Jail,** now being restored as a museum, open from 1500 to 1700, Sundays only, admission 5p for adults, 3p for children.

THEATRE No theatres have regular matinees but during the pantomime season in January and February, and the summer variety shows, there are often children's matinees at reduced prices on Saturday afternoon.

CINEMA Children are admitted at half-price to afternoon showings of films. There is no graded certificate system as in Britain, but some films are restricted to audiences over-12, over-16, over-18 and even over-21, though these restrictions are not vigorously enforced. The system of censorship which operates inevitably bans or cuts films with any degree of sex content, regardless of the film's cinematic qualities, but often allows the very youngest of children to see violent and brutal films. Some suburban cinemas have special children's matinees on Saturday or Sunday afternoons, at either 1400 or 1500. The show is made up of a combination of cartoons, serials and family adventure films. Among the cinemas are the **De Luxe,** Camden Street, the **New Sandford,** Ranelagh, the **Star,** Crumlin, the **Ormonde,** Stillorgan, the **Kenilworth,** Harold's Cross Road. Details of times and programmes are in Friday's and Saturday's evenings newspapers.

EDUCATIONAL TOURS There are a number of industrial undertakings which accept tours of students and school-children, and visits are arranged by the Student representative, Student Travel Department, **Dublin Tourism,** 51 Dawson Street, Dublin 2. Tel. 47733

The regulations vary according to the undertaking; special visits to **Dunsink Observatory,** Castleknock, to study the instruments can only be arranged for University Science students; **An Foras Talúntais** (Agricultural Institute), Dunsinea, Castleknock, would only be of interest to university students or sixth formers considering a career in agricultural science, veterinary medicine or biochemistry, and **Core Memories** can only be visited by University Science and Engineering students. Other firms impose minimum age restrictions; for example, at **Guinness Brewery,** St James's Gate, no children under 12 are admitted; at **Irish Distillers,** the minimum age is 17; at **Unidare,** 14, and other firms require advance notice ranging from 3 days for **Solus Teo** in Bray to 2 weeks for **Pye (Ireland)** and **Gouldings Chemicals. Leo Laboratories,** Cashel Road, have an age limit of 16–17 years; their tour lasts one hour and is followed by tea and a film show. The **Irish Hospitals Sweepstakes,** Ballsbridge, is open for tours from 0900 to 1200 and 1400 to 1700 each day, and souvenirs of glass and ashtrays are available. Needless to say there is no charge for the above-mentioned tours.

TELEVISION AND RADIO There are children's programmes, usually between 1700 and 1800 on weekdays, and during the school term there are educational programmes on television beginning at 1030.

TRANSPORT **Bicycles** are the cheapest and handiest form of transport, with the reservation that cyclists are in daily confrontation with some of the most reckless driving seen outside of Italy. Children are entitled to reduced fares on public transport—*see* **Buses.**

STUDENTS IN DUBLIN

FREE Dublin hardly exists, but cheap Dublin is possible if you look hard enough, and you should certainly be able to live on less than the proverbial $5 a day. This section is not intended exclusively for students but hopefully will be of use to any young person trying to live in what has recently become a very expensive city.

WHERE TO SLEEP

For a long stay in the city, **flats, apartments** or **bedsitters** are by far the cheapest and most pleasant. Prices vary considerably, depending on facilities, but even more important, the area you choose. North of the Liffey is invariably cheaper, Ballsbridge the most expensive area, with Ranelagh and Rathmines in between. The weekly rent for a single bedsitter varies between £4.50 and £11.00. It is cheaper to share, and the more the better; 4 people should get a 2-bedroomed flat for between £11.00 and £14.00 a week. However the larger and more expensive the flat, the greater the likelihood that you will have to sign a 6-month or 1-year lease. As a rule you must give, and are entitled to receive, notice to quit on the same time-scale as the rent is paid, i.e. rent paid by the week—one week's notice either way; paid by the month, one month's notice. For the more expensive flats a separate refundable deposit against damage is often required; for bedsitters and cheaper flats a week's rent in advance is more usual. Unless the apartment has a coin box electricity meter, you will have to pay the Electricity Supply Board, Fleet Street, a £5.00 deposit, refundable when you leave; allow about 5 days for the electricity to be connected. The larger estate agents such as **Lisney's,** 23 St Stephen's Green, tel. 64471, and **Osborne, King and Megran,** 32 Molesworth Street, tel. 60251, have lists of what is currently available, though they tend to be of the expensive type. The most complete list is to be found in the accommodation section of the *Evening Press,* especially Mondays and Thursdays, early editions available in the city centre from about 1445. The *Irish Times* also carries a shorter list of flats available. There is widespread discrimination against students, male students, long-haired students, non-white students, and married couples in that order. October is the worst month for flat-hunting, June the best. Hundreds of Dublin students leave their flats during the summer, so you may be able to reduce the landlord's asking price during this period.

HOSTELS **An Oige,** the Irish Youth Hostel Association, has two hostels, at 39 Mountjoy Square, tel. 45734 (72 beds) and 78 Morehampton Road, Dublin 4, tel. 680325 (80 beds). There are cooking facilities. Accommodation is available to male and female members of an affiliated Youth Hostel Association, and your stay is restricted to 3 consecutive nights if there is a waiting list; it is advisable to book in advance. You must leave the hostel by 1030 and be in at night by 2300. The cost for those over 21 is 35p per night, under 21, 30p.

The **Y.W.C.A.** 64 Lower Baggot Street, Dublin 2, tel. 66273, has accommodation for girls, ranging from 60p to £1.00 a night including breakfast. **Trinity Hall,** the women's hall of residence attached to Trinity College, at Dartry, Dublin 6, tel. 971772, often has accommodation available during the summer months for girls only.

For men there is the **Salvation Army Men's Hostel,** York Street, Dublin 2, tel. 754039, with an individual cubicle and breakfast for 35p per night. The **Morning Star Hostel,** North Brunsworth Street, Dublin 7, tel. 776083, is a hostel 'for necessitous men' where supper, bed and breakfast are provided at a nominal fee, and there are also showers, television and recreational facilities. Undoubtedly the cheapest hostel is the **Dublin Corporation Lodging House,** Benburb Street, Dublin 7, tel. 770689, where 'adult males of good health and character who are in need of shelter' can have a cubicle, television, cooking facilities and showers, all for 5p a night. Needless to say none of these establishments could be described as luxurious, but since in some cases they are about one hundredth of the price of a hotel bedroom, they are certainly good value. If you are sleeping rough, the 1,760 acres of **Phoenix Park** offers the most possibilities, but your sleep could be disturbed by the police. Sleeping-bags cost about 75p a week to hire, ground sheets 40p a week, air mattress with pump 80p and two-bedroomed chalet tent for four about £8.00 a week, from **O'Meara Camping**, 160A Crumlin Road, Dublin 12, tel. 52315/16, or **Irish Camping**, 33 Leeson Close, Lower Leeson Street, Dublin 2, tel. 67186. The two nearest camp sites are **Rent-a-Sprite**, Sherrindon Park, Shankill, Co. Dublin, tel. 863006, and **Cromlech Cottage Caravan and Tent Park,** Killiney Hill Road, near Ballybrack, tel. 804562.

WHERE TO EAT

At home preferably, or in your flat or hostel; as a rule few restaurants in Dublin are cheap or good value. If you are shopping for food try the **street markets** in **Camden Street** or **Moore Street** off Henry Street for vegetables, fruit, fish and meat; here they are at least one third cheaper than in the suburban shop or supermarket. Certain grocers give a 5 per cent or 10 per cent reduction to students on production of a student card; among them are **Fitzpatrick's**, **Russell's** and the **Bounty Stores**, all in Camden Street, and **Corrigan's** and **Paddy's Supermarket** in Wexford Street. Just as important as where to eat is what to eat—choose **one main meal a day;** for visitors and sight-seers, a large Irish breakfast is probably the most appropriate. If lunch is to be your main meal, steer clear of most pubs, except perhaps the **Stag's Head** or **Stag's Tail,** in Dame Court. The Chinese restaurants serve a good-value three-course lunch for about 32½p for soup, choice of four main dishes, two Chinese and two European, and dessert, usually ice-cream. For an evening meal look for a traditional Irish High Tea; mixed grill with a pot of tea and as much brown bread or soda bread as you can eat. Eating facilities in the universities include the **Buttery** in **Trinity College** for light snacks (non-Trinity students usually refused service in the Academic year) and **Newman House,** 86 St Stephen's Green, for **University College.** Lunch in the **Graduates Restaurant** in Newman House is good value, open between 1230 and 1430. The basement restaurant opens from 1000 to 1800, and until 1400 on Saturdays. Simple fare but reasonable value. For a low-priced meal in the late evening, **Gaj's** of Baggot Street offers tasty snacks and interesting company.

WHERE TO DRINK

Students from the two universities have separate drinking areas, though they overlap somewhat along Merrion Row, where **Toner's, Nesbitt's** and **O'Donoghue's** (for traditional music) are the most popular. Trinity students use the **Suffolk House,** Suffolk Street; **Lincoln Inn**, Lincoln Place, the **College Mooney** in College Street, and **O'Neill's** in Suffolk Street. Most of the students attending University College Dublin have been moved to the new campus in Belfield, but drinking patterns are not as easily shifted, and the Lower Leeson Street area is still the most popular haunt. **Hartigan's** is traditionally for medical students and rugby players; girls and law students admitted grudgingly. Across the road, **McDermott's** which will always be known as **Kirwan's** is still something of an unknown quantity. In its former existence, **Kirwan's** used to attract law students and a mixture of all the other faculties. The most popular is **O'Dwyer's** packed to capacity most times of the day, most days of the week. The upstairs lounge attracts the younger crowd and the bikeys, downstairs caters for recent and not so recent graduates. The barmen are the very best and friendliest in Dublin, which is a good enough reason for putting up with the crowds and discomfort.

WHERE TO SMOKE

Not in public. Dublin is a small intimate city; hard and soft drugs are easily available—but so are you to the efficient and hardworking Drug Squad. They are particularly firm with pushers. There is a 24-hour drug advisory service attached to **Jervis Street Hospital,** Dublin 1. Tel. 48412.

FREE FOOD

A number of Dublin convents run free food centres, serving either breakfasts, lunches, teas and sometimes all three. Though it is unlikely that the good sisters would refuse food to anyone, the service is intended for those genuinely poor and hungry, **not** for the international (so-called) hippies whose pockets bulge with travellers cheques.

Among the centres are **St Agnes Convent,** Armagh Road, Crumlin, Dublin 12; **St Brigid's,** Holles Row, Dublin 2; **St Mary Magdalene,** Donnybrook (men only), the **Sisters of Charity,** Mount St Annes, Milltown, and **St Joseph's,** North Cumberland Street, Dublin 1.

WHERE TO SHOP

CLOTHES   As a general rule stay away from the Grafton Street area where goods can cost twice as much as in the shops in Henry Street, Talbot Street, Great George's Street or Camden Street. Certain shops give reductions to students who produce a recognised student card. This type of shop or store should have a green and white USI sticker in the window. The two trendiest of men's boutiques, **Adam** and **Jeffson,** both in Duke Lane, offer a 7½ per cent reduction, their clothes are good, particularly in the latter, but prices are expensive to start with. **Murphy's** 6 D'Olier Street, offer a 15 per cent reduction on their clothes, **Bryson's** the tailor's, 3 Church Lane, College Green, **Elvery's,** Dawson Street, and **Woodrow's,** O'Connell Bridge House, all offer reductions for student card holders. For girls' clothes there are discounts for students at **Caroline's,** 16 Wicklow Street, **Ambush Boutique** in the Grafton Arcade, **It's a Beautiful Day,** Duke Lane, and all branches of **Mamie's** (in the George's Street and Henry Street arcades, and the Stillorgan and Rathfarnham shopping centres). For footwear, **Pick-a-shoe,** 19 Camden Street, offers 10 per cent off, and **O'Neill's** of Talbot Street and branches of **Cripp's** offer 5 per cent off.

JEWELLERS **Yeates and Son,** the **Grafton Jewellers,** and **West's,** all in Grafton Street, **Tiffany's,** 11 Andrew Street, and **John Morton,** 48 Nassau Street, offer a reduction to students.

WINES AND SPIRITS **Donlan Bros,** 57 Moore Street, offer a reduction on grocery, wines, spirits and cigarettes.

PHOTOGRAPHERS AND EQUIPMENT **Lafayette's,** 22 Westmoreland Street, offer a 20 per cent reduction to students; **Graphic Studios,** 74 Lower Camden Street, and **Dick Garvin,** 1 St Stephen's Green, offer a 10 per cent reduction. Among the photographic equipment shops with reductions are **Dixon Hempenstall,** 111 Grafton Street, the **Camera Centre,** 9 Burgh Quay, and the **Camera Shop,** 69 Parnell Square.

MOTORBIKES, CYCLES, ETC. **McHugh Himself,** 39 Talbot Street, gives $12\frac{1}{2}$ per cent discount; the **Motor Shop,** Stillorgan Shopping Centre, and the **Accessory Centre,** 107 Rathmines Road, give a 10 per cent reduction.

RECORDS AND TAPES, ETC. **Pat Egan's Sound Cellar,** 49 Nassau Street, **Tara Record Centre,** Tara Street, and **Discfinder,** 147 Lower Baggot Street, have reductions for students. **Discfinder** is open until 2200 on Wednesdays and Fridays.

FLORISTS **Marie Jeanne,** 24 Dawson Street has a $12\frac{1}{2}$ per cent reduction and **Floriana,** 26 Dawson Street, a 10 per cent reduction for student card holders.

DRESS HIRE **Murphy's** of D'Olier Street offer a 15 per cent reduction; **Peter Jansen,** 3 Lower Pembroke Street charge 87p instead of the normal cost of £1.37½p.

117

DRIVING LESSONS **St Christopher School of Motoring,** 15 Warrington Place, tel. 62501, has a 10 per cent reduction on each lesson.

ANTIQUES **Sheeran's,** 25 Bachelor's Walk and **Patrick Oman** of Dandelion Green (an antique hyper-market on St Stephen's Green) are among the dealers which give reductions to students. Others are **City Antiques,** Dawson Street, **Anthony Antiques,** Molesworth Street, and **Matthews,** Merchants Arch, off Aston Quay.

HAIRDRESSERS For girls, **McDonald's,** 1 St Stephen's Green, has a 20 per cent reduction for students, and the **House of Claude** and **Tudor Rooms** also in Stephen's Green have a special reduction. In Grafton Street, **Maison Frank** and **House of Paul** have a reduced price for students. For men, **Ernest Mallon,** 7 College Street, and **T. O'Connor** of Westmoreland Street offer a 10 per cent reduction to students.

DRY-CLEANING The **Madrid Cleaners** have a 25 per cent reduction for students; the **Grafton Cleaners,** Grafton street, **Lyk-nu,** Stephen's Green, **Marlborough Cleaners,** Talbot Street and **Marlowe's** in Westmoreland Street offer 10 per cent off.

HEALTH The **Grafton Health Studio,** Grafton Street, offers a 15 per cent reduction to students.

WHERE TO RELAX

Theatre in Dublin is all too relaxing and comfortable at least in the artistic sense; the **Abbey** has about 90 seats at reduced prices (25p) for students from Monday to Wednesdays, September to May, and a smaller number available during the summer. The **Peacock,** below the Abbey, is usually more adventurous, and occasionally presents experimental plays at lunchtime, coffee and sandwiches served. Directly opposite the Peacock is the **Project**

Arts Centre, an artists' co-operative gallery which also caters for theatre, music and poetry. There is usually something happening each weekend—call in or telephone 40282. The **Davis** gallery, Capel Street, normally shows exhibitions of the work of young Irish artists. **Cinema** in Dublin is cheap, particularly in the suburbs, but all films shown publicly can be censored and cut, and frequently are. For further details *see* **Cinema** section. The number and quality of **discothèques** fluctuates quite regularly, and since many of them may have closed or changed management, only the briefest details are given. Most have restaurant facilities and a wine licence, and the cover charge varies from 40p to 70p. In addition there is often an annual membership charge, usually 50p, though the membership requirement may be waived for visitors, particularly earlier in the week, when the discos are less likely to be crowded. One of the longest established is **Le Disque,** 5 Molesworth Street, open till 0200 Sunday to Friday and to 0300 on Saturday. **Jonathan's** downstairs is open until 0200 every night except Sunday; last meals are served at 0015 and there is no cover charge. The **Zhivago Club,** 15 Baggot Street, **Sloopy's,** 17 Fleet Street, **The Revolution,** 5 Rutland Place, **Tiffany's,** 12 Chapel Lane behind Roches and **Seezer's,** 30 Upper Abbey Street, are all big discothèques, which combine or alternate record nights with rock groups. They open between 2100 and 2200 and continue to 0200 or 0300 each day. For something completely different, sample the unique Irish **show-band** scene. These seven to ten-piece bands are possibly the closest thing to the Swing Sound of the forties. The showbands are especially popular outside Dublin, but you can hear them in the city too. Many of the musicians are extremely talented, professional and versatile, playing pop, ballads, folk, but their staple diet is country and western—though it is country and western Irish-style which too often means trite, sentimental, mother-fixated lyrics sung to maudlin derivative tunes. But each to his own. . . . You can see and hear the showbands in action at the

119

Olympic, Pleasants Street, the **Television Club,** Harcourt Street, the **Ierne Ballroom** and the **National Ballroom,** Parnell Square, the **Crystal,** South Anne Street, and the **Town and Country Club,** Cavendish Row, which is beside the Gate Theatre. Admission is usually about 50p or 60p.

INFORMATION

Apart from the usual sources such as newspapers, tourist offices, etc., most information concerning rock concerts, poetry readings, plays, protest demonstrations, etc., is communicated by poster. None of it is in the Toulouse-Lautrec league, but the style is improving.

TRANSPORT

Most of the city is easily accessible on foot, but for the cheapest form of transport *see* **Bicycles.** For cheap bicycles check with the local Garda (Police) station, for the date of the annual lost property auction, when you can pick up a good bicycle for a few pounds. For **foreign travel,** contact **Irish Student Travel Service,** 11 St Stephen's Green, for cheap student flights to Europe, North America, Africa or the Far East.

DUBLIN DATA

CLIMATE

DUBLIN has a maritime climate—mild winters and cool summers. January is the coldest month with a mean temperature of 4.5°C (40°F), and July and August are the warmest with a mean temperature of about 15°C (59°F). The relative humidity is normally between 70 and 90 per cent.

Month	Average Temperature	Rainfall (Millimetres)	Hours of Sunshine
January	4·5°C	67	59
February	4·9°C	55	71
March	6·5°C	51	104
April	8·2°C	45	151
May	10·7°C	60	192
June	13·8°C	57	180
July	15·3°C	70	148
August	15·0°C	74	152
September	13·1°C	72	118
October	10·1°C	70	98
November	7·1°C	67	63
December	5·5°C	75	49

MONEY MATTERS

Banking hours are weekdays 1000 to 1230 and 1330 to 1500 (and 1700 on Thursdays). Closed on Saturdays, Sundays and bank holidays.

FOREIGN EXCHANGE Travellers cheques and foreign currency can be cashed in most banks, and travellers cheques and well-known foreign currencies are accepted in most hotels, large shops and travel companies. The **American Express** office is at : 116 Grafton Street, Dublin 2. Tel. 772874

Thomas Cook is at 118 Grafton Street, Dublin 2. Tel. 771721

Since most currencies are 'floating' on the international money market it is not possible to give an exact currency guide but the following table gives the approximate exchange rates :

ITALY		AUSTRIA	
50 Lire =	3p	10 Schillings =	16p
100 Lire =	6p	50 Schillings =	80p
500 Lire =	30p	100 Schillings =	£1·60p
5,000 Lire =	£3·25p		

PORTUGAL		BELGIUM	
10 Escudos =	14p	10 Francs =	9p
50 Escudos =	70p	50 Francs =	45p
100 Escudos =	£1.40p	100 Francs =	90p

SPAIN		CANADA	
10 Pesetas =	6p	1 Dollar =	39p
50 Pesetas =	30p	10 Dollar =	£3·90p
100 Pesetas =	60p		

SWEDEN		FRANCE	
1 Kronor =	8p	1 Franc =	7p
10 Kronor =	80p	10 Franc =	70p
100 Kronor =	£8·00p	100 Franc =	£7·00p

SWITZERLAND		GERMANY	
1 Franc =	10p	1 Deutchesmark =	12p
10 Franc =	£1·00p	10 Deutchesmark =	£1·20p
		50 Deutchesmark =	£6·00p

U.S.A.		HOLLAND	
1 Dollar =	39p	1 Guilder =	12p
10 Dollar =	£3·90p	10 Guilder =	£1·20p
		50 Guilder =	£6·00p

POST OFFICES

The **General Post Office** is at Lower O'Connell Street, tel. 48888. Open for sale of stamps, acceptance of telegrams, registered and express letters each day from 0800 to 2300. On Sundays, open from 1000 (except for telegrams, open from 09.00). For all other business the G.P.O. is open from 0800 to 2000 except Sundays. **Poste Restante :** facilities available from 0800 to 2000 including Sundays and bank holidays.

OTHER POST OFFICES

Andrew Street
Tel. 778621   Monday to Saturday   0830 to 1830
South Anne Street
Tel. 777127   „   „   „   0900 to 1800
James Street
Tel. 777174   „   „   „   0900 to 1800
Ballsbridge
Tel. 684979   „   „   „   0900 to 1800
Phibsboro
Tel. 304142   „   „   „   0900 to 1800
Rathmines
Tel. 972319   „   „   „   0900 to 1800

There are 3 daily postal deliveries for letters in the city centre on weekdays and none on Saturday or Sunday, though letters sent 'Express' will be delivered on Saturday mornings. There are 2 postal deliveries each day in the suburbs, and none on Saturday and Sunday.

TELEPHONES

It is almost impossible to describe just how bad the Irish telephone system really is. What in other countries has become one of the basic means of communication, still remains an adventure in Ireland, with the cards stacked firmly against the telephone user. In theory at least, making a local telephone call is very simple : when you hear the dial tone, insert a 2p coin or two 1p coins, dial the number required, and when your call is answered press button A, and begin your 3 minutes-worth of conversation. In practice, however, you will require a great deal of luck, patience and usually more than the appropriate 2p. Out of ten attempts to call from a public phone box, you are likely to find four of the booths smashed by vandals, three simply out of order, and one where the coin box has not been emptied, so that either you are unable to fit any money in, or having fitted it, you cannot get a refund if there is no reply to your call. One more call is likely to lead to a crossed line—too late—you have pressed button A and so have lost another 2p. With luck on your side, your tenth attempt may be successful, provided of course that the other person's phone is not out of order as well. It is little compensation to find that the telephone operators, when they do manage to answer the phone, are for the most part courteous and sympathetic—after all sympathy is about all they can offer. Nor is it a solution to limit yourself to private phones, where lines become crossed even more frequently—and anyway you will have to wait 6 to 9 months (not hours as in the U.S.) with the other 18,000 hopefuls for a private phone to be installed. Occasionally the balance is corrected in your favour, when you press button B after yet another abortive attempt, to be showered by thirty or forty coins as though you had hit the jackpot on a slot machine! If you do have to telephone, the most practical solution is to seek out a good hotel or large department store such as **Brown Thomas** or **Switzer's,** and have the switchboard operator make the call. The charge will be about 9p but this apparent extravagance will save you time, tranquillisers and probably some money as well.

Apart from the actual business of providing telephone communication, the service is quite good. Among the ancillary services are :

Weather Forecast	Dial 1199	Local call fee
Time Service (Speaking Clock)	Dial 1191	Local call fee
Alarm Clock Call	Dial 10	5p private phone
		7p call box
Emergency (Police, Ambulance, Fire Brigade)	Dial 999	No charge
Directory Enquiries	Dial 190	No charge
Telephone Faults (a very useful number)	191	No charge

elephone Service and other		
quiries	Dial 199	No charge
elegrams (from private		
one)	Dial 115	
runk Calls	Dial 10	
ersonal Trunk Calls	Dial 10	Additional charge of 10p.
xed Time Trunk Call	Dial 10	Additional charge, calculated at the rate of $\frac{1}{4}$ the charge of a 3-minute call.
aily Fixed Time Trunk Call	Dial 10	Additional charge calculated at the rate of $\frac{1}{8}$ the charge of a 3-minute call.
D.C. (Advice of Duration		
d Charge)	Dial 10	Additional charge of 5p.
rect Dial to **London**	Prefix 031	
rect Dial to **Belfast**	Prefix 084	

There is a reduction of between 25 per cent and 33 per
nt for trunk calls at certain times :

1. For internal trunk calls and calls to Northern Ireland
d the United Kingdom, between 1800 to 0800 each day.

2. For the United States (excluding Alaska and Hawaii)
d Canada, between 2200 and 1000 (Irish Time) and all
y Sunday.

Reversed Charges (i.e. 'calling collect') are only accepted
r U.S.A. and Mexico.

ther Emergency Phone Numbers

maritans : Tel. 754254. 24-hour confidential service for
e lonely depressed and suicidal.

lcoholics Anonymous : Tel. 977656

DRY-CLEANING

Hour Service

rafton Cleaners, 22 Grafton Street, Dublin 2

co, 4 Talbot Street, Dublin 1

co, 30 Grafton Street, Dublin 2

co, 21 Nassau Street, Dublin 2

co, 132 St Stephen's Green, Dublin 2

ic and Span Cleaners, 81 Camden Street, Dublin 2

viss Cleaners, 112 Thomas Street, Dublin 8

vift Cleaners, 62/63 Middle Abbey Street, Dublin 1

2 HOUR SERVICE

New York Pressing & Cleaning, 68 & 83 Middle Abbey
    Street, Dublin 1

Prescotts Cleaners & Dyers, 82 Talbot Street, Dublin 1

4 HOUR SERVICE

Marlow Cleaners, 28 Westmoreland Street, Dublin 2
      ,,   ,,   38 Lower Camden Street, Dublin 2
      ,,   ,,   90 South Great George's Street, Dublin 2
      ,,   ,,   58 Upper O'Connell Street, Dublin 1
      ,,   ,,   28 Capel Street, Dublin 1
      ,,   ,,   103 Terenure Road, Dublin 6
Dartry Cleaners, 141 Lower Baggot Street, Dublin 2
      ,,   ,,   45 Dawson Street, Dublin 2
Streamline Cleaners, 7 Cathedral Street, Dublin 1

OFF-LICENCES (AND WINE SHOPS)

McGuinness, 89 Phibsboro Road, Dublin 7. Tel. 301218

MacGowan's, 27 Carysfort Avenue, Blackrock. Tel. 881649

Italian Wine Shop, beside **Unicorn Restaurant,** off Merrion
    Row, Dublin 2

Bartley Dunnes, 32 Lower Stephen Street. Tel. 753137
    (A very wide range including Chinese and Greek wines)

Smyths of the Green, 6 St Stephen's Green, Dublin 2
    Tel. 770131

Searsons, 33 South Richmond Street, Dublin 2. Tel. 757136

Redmonds, 25 Ranelagh Road, Dublin 6. Tel. 971739

Donlon's, 57/58 Moore Street, Dublin 1. Tel. 44198

Dublin Wine Society, 13 Fitzwilliam Square, Dublin 1
    Tel. 65964

Most off-licences are attached to grocery stores or public
houses, and the sale of alcohol follows the normal licensing
hours.

SAUNA BATHS

Ranelagh Health Institute, 47 Ranelagh Road, Dublin 6. Tel. 974325

The Nerve Clinic, 6 Upper Fitzwilliam Street, Dublin 2. Tel. 65638

Lansdowne Hotel, Pembroke Road, Dublin 4. Tel. 62549

Hotel Montrose, Stillorgan Road, Dublin 4. Tel. 694095

Eurocentre, 63A South Great George's Street, Dublin 2. Tel. 758424

Grafton Health Studio, Creation House, Grafton Street, Dublin 2. Tel. 771405

LAUNDERETTES AND WASHETERIAS

Coin-op Centre, 46 Upper Baggot Street, Dublin 4. Tel. 600006

Snow White Launderette, 13 Ranelagh Road, Dublin 6. Tel. 971935

The Speedy Laundromat, 19 Aungier Street, Dublin 2. Tel. 756297

Washeteria, 101 Parnell Street, Dublin 1. Tel. 47534

Washeteria, 110 Dorset Street, Dublin 1. Tel. 305071

There are many others in the suburbs, and most are open 0900 to 2030 6 days a week. Charges vary but the use of a larger washing machine usually costs about 20p, and drying is 5p. If you prefer it, you can have your clothes washed and dried for you for a small extra charge, usually about 10p.

GUIDE SERVICES

Take-a-Guide, 13 Nutley Road, Dublin 4. Tel. 691811. Car included in the service, shopping tour, Yeats' or Joyce's Dublin, and county Dublin included. Cost is about £5.00 for $2\frac{1}{2}$ hours, between £6.00 and £8.00 for a half-day. **Askus,** 19 Duke Street, Dublin 2. Tel. 779954. Guide only, but interpreter service included; £4 for a half day, £7.50 for a full day.

Curran Guides, 4 Lower Leeson Street, Dublin 2. Tel. 66198. £6.00 per day anywhere.

INTERPRETER AND TRANSLATION SERVICES

Dublin Interpreter Services, 44 Gifford Road, Sandymount, Dublin 4. Tel. 692858. Professional and business conference services. Main European languages. **Askus,** 19 Duke Street, Dublin 2. Tel. 779954. Translation and interpreting. All European languages and Russian, Japanese and Chinese. **Translation rate :** 80p per 100 words, £8.00 per 1,000 words for European languages; £10.00 per 1,000 words for others.

LOCKSMITHS

Broderick's, 21 Dawson Street, Dublin 2. Tel. 61671. Mobile locksmiths on call.

Devine's, 19 South King Street, Dublin 2. Tel. 752561

Fogarty's, 5 Crane Lane, Dublin 2. Tel. 771961

Woolworths, Grafton Street and Henry Street. Keys cut while you wait.

24-HOUR LOCKSMITHS **J. Williams,** 130 Mercer Street, Dublin 2. Tel. 756307 from 0900 to 1730. After 1800 and weekends, tel, 776988. House calls at awkward hours of the night will be made, but it could cost about £5.00, so you have to assess whether your front door (or shoulder) is worth that much.

LATE NIGHT SHOPS

A number of small grocery shops, mainly in the suburbs, stay open till midnight or later. **Muldoons,** Ranelagh Road, Ranelagh, is open till midnight every night, and stocks all the main groceries. **Campbells,** 63 Upper Rathmines Road, and the **Leinster Chalet,** Lower Rathmines Road, stay open till 0100 or later, and at weekends till 0200 or 0300. **Cosgroves Chicken Shop** in Terenure, which also sells delicatessen products, is open till 2330. **D&B** of Lower Baggot Street, better known as 'Dollies', is open until 2300.

CHEMIST SHOPS

Most chemist shops are open from 0900 to 1800 or 1900 Monday to Saturday. Certain suburban chemist shops open on Sundays from 1100 to 1300. If a chemist shop does not open on Sunday it will display a notice indicating which chemist shop is open in the area.

ALL-NIGHT CHEMIST SHOPS There is no rota system of all-night chemists as such. In certain suburbs where the proprietor of a chemist's lives over the premises, he will make up urgent doctor's prescriptions. There is no such service in Rathfarnham, Rathgar, Terenure, Templeogue, but there are chemist shops at Kimmage Road West, Walkinstown Cross, Foxrock, Stillorgan, Crumlin and Ranelagh (Johnston's, 21 Ranelagh Road) which offer this service. Remember very urgent prescriptions only.

CHURCHES AND SERVICES

All the churches listed below are indicated on *The Essential Map of Dublin,* at the end of the book, by the symbol ✚ and the number which appears in brackets after the name of each church on the following list.

ROMAN CATHOLIC

Pro-Cathedral (1), Marlborough Street
St Andrew's (2), Westland Row
St Audoen's (3), High Street
St Joseph's (4), Berkeley Road
St Kevin's (5) Harrington Street
St Columba's (6), Iona Road, Glasnevin
Corpus Christi (7), Griffith Avenue, Drumcondra
St Mary's (8), Haddington Road
St Francis Xavier (9), Upper Gardiner Street (Jesuit)
St Paul's (10), Arran Quay
St Peter's (11) Phibsboro
St John the Baptist (12), Thomas Street (St John's Lane)
(Augustinian)
Our Lady of Mount Carmel (13), Whitefriar Street
(Carmelite)

St Teresa's (14), Clarendon Street (Carmelite)
St Saviour's (15), Dominick Street (Dominican)
St Mary of the Angels (16), Church Street (Franciscan/ Capuchin)
The Immaculate Conception (17), Merchants' Quay (Franciscan)
University Church (18), St Stephen's Green
SS Michael & John (19), Lower Exchange Street
City Quay (20)
Blessed Sacrament Chapel (21), D'Olier Street

Sunday Mass is usually celebrated on the hour or half-hour, but as the following time schedule indicates, you can attend Mass at almost forty different times in the selection of Catholic churches listed above.

0500	The Immaculate Conception
0530	Our Lady of Mount Carmel; St Teresa's
0600	St Francis Xavier; St Mary of the Angels; The Immaculate Conception
0615	Our Lady of Mount Carmel; St Teresa's
0630	Pro-Cathedral; St Francis Xavier
0700	St Andrews; St Joseph's; Corpus Christi; St Mary's (Haddington Road); St Francis Xavier; St Peter's; Our Lady of Mount Carmel; St Teresa's; St Mary of the Angels; The Immaculate Conception
0730	Pro-Cathedral; St Andrew's; St Kevin's (Irish); St Columba's (Irish); St John the Baptist; St Saviour's
0745	St Francis Xavier; Our Lady of Mount Carmel; St Teresa's
0800	St Audoen's; St Joseph's; Corpus Christi; St Mary's (Haddington Road); St Paul's (Irish); St Peter's; St Mary of the Angels; The Immaculate Conception; University Church; SS Michael & John; City Quay; Blessed Sacrament
0815	Pro-Cathedral (Irish)
0830	St Andrew's; St Kevin's; St Columba's; St Francis Xavier; St John the Baptist; Our Lady of Mount Carmel; St Teresa's; St Saviour's

0845	St Mary's (Haddington Road)
0900	Pro-Cathedral; St Andrew's; St Joseph's;
0900	Pro-Cathedral; St Andrew's; St Joseph's; Corpus Christi (Irish); St Paul's; St Peter's; St Mary of the Angels; The Immaculate Conception; University Church (Irish); SS Michael & John; City Quay
0915	St Francis Xavier; St John The Baptist; Our Lady of Mount Carmel; St Teresa's
0930	St Andrew's; St Kevin's; St Columba's; St Mary's (Haddington Road) (Irish); St Saviour's
0945	Pro-Cathedral
1000	St Audoen's; St Joseph's (Irish); Corpus Christi; St Francis Xavier; St Paul's; St Peter's; St John the Baptist; Our Lady of Mount Carmel; St Teresa's (Irish); St Mary of the Angels; The Immaculate Conception; University Church; SS Michael & John; City Quay; Blessed Sacrament
1015	St Mary's (Haddington Road)
1030	Pro-Cathedral; St Andrew's; St Kevin's; St Columba's; St Saviour's
1045	St Audoen's; St Joseph's; Corpus Christi; St Francis Xavier; St Paul's; St John the Baptist; Our Lady of Mount Carmel; St Teresa's; St Mary of the Angels; The Immaculate Conception; University Church; SS Michael & John; City Quay
1100	St Mary's (Haddington Road); Blessed Sacrament
1115	Pro-Cathedral
1130	St Andrew's; St Audoen's; St Joseph's; St Kevin's; St Columba's; Corpus Christi; St Francis Xavier; St Paul's; St John the Baptist; Our Lady of Mount Carmel; St Teresa's; St Saviour; The Immaculate Conception; University Church; SS Michael & John; City Quay
1145	St Mary's (Haddington Road)
1200	Pro-Cathedral; St Peter's; Blessed Sacrament
1215	St Joseph's; Corpus Christi; St Francis Xavier; St Paul's; St John the Baptist; Our Lady of Mount

Carmel; St Teresa's; The Immaculate Conception; SS Michael & John; City Quay

1230	St Andrew's; St Columba's; St Mary's (Haddington Road); St Saviour's
1235	Pro-Cathedral (High Mass)
1245	St Audoen's; Blessed Sacrament
1300	St Peter's
1730	St Audoen's; St Columba's; Corpus Christi; St Francis Xavier; St Saviour's
1745	Pro-Cathedral
1800	St Mary's (Haddington Road); St Peter's (October to March)
1900	Pro-Cathedral; St Andrew's; St Joseph's; St Francis Xavier; St Paul's; Our Lady of Mount Carmel; St Teresa's; City Quay
1930	St John the Baptist; The Immaculate Conception
2000	Blessed Sacrament; St Peter's (April to September)
2030	St Saviour's
2100	SS Michael & John

Foreign Language Confessions : Pro-Cathedral : Italian and Spanish; Donnybrook : French, Italian, German, Spanish.

CHURCH OF IRELAND

Christchurch Cathedral (22), Christchurch Place
Sunday, Matins & Holy Communion 1100; Evensong 1500.
St Patrick's Cathedral (23), Patrick Street
Sunday, Holy Communion 0830; Matins 1115; Evensong 1515.
St Andrew's (24), Suffolk Street
Sunday, Matins & Holy Communion 1130; Evensong 1900.
St Anne's (25), Dawson Street
Sunday, Holy Communion 0800; Matins 1015 & 1130; Evensong 1900.
St Bartholomew's (26), Clyde Road, Ballsbridge
Sunday, The Eucharist 0800 & 0915; Matins & Sermon 1100; Sung Eucharist 1200; Evensong & Service.

St George's (27), Temple Street
Sunday, Holy Communion 0800; Morning Prayer 1100.
St Mary's (29), Mary Street
Sunday, Morning Prayer & Holy Communion 1015.
St Thomas's, Cathal Brugha Street
Sunday, Morning Prayer and Holy Communion 1015.

PRESBYTERIAN
Abbey Church (30), Parnell Square
Sunday, 1130 and 1900 winter; 1100 and 2030 June and
September
Lower Abbey Street (31), Sunday, 1130 and 1900
Adelaide Road (32), Sunday, 1100 and 1900
Christ Church (33), Rathgar. Sunday, 1100 and 1900
Tritonville Road (34), Sandymount. Sunday, 1130 and
1900

METHODIST
Lower Abbey Street Central Mission (35). Sunday 1130
and 1900
Centenary Church (36), St Stephen's Green. Sunday, 1130
and 1900
Sandymount Green (37) Sandymount. Sunday 1130 and
1900

JEWISH
(Services on Saturdays at 0900)
Terenure Synagogue (38), Rathfarnham Road
Greenville Hall Synagogue (39), South Circular Road
Adelaide Road Synagogue (53)

PROGRESSIVE
Leicester Avenue (40), Rathgar. Friday 2000; Saturday
1000.

CHRISTIAN SCIENCE
Second Church of Christ Scientist (42), Rathmines Park.
Sunday, 1130 and 1900

BAPTIST
Grosvenor Road (43), Rathgar. Sunday, 1130 and 1900
Phibsboro (44), Sunday, 1130 and 1900

UNITARIAN
St Stephen's Green (45). Sunday, 1130 and 1930

MORAVIAN,
16 St Stephen's Green

CONGREGATIONAL
Inchicore Road (47), Kilmainham. Sunday, 1130 and 1900

LUTHERAN
St Finian's (48), 83 Adelaide Road. Sunday, 1100

SOCIETY OF FRIENDS
Eustace Street (49). Sunday, 1100

SEVENTH DAY ADVENTIST
47A Ranelagh Road (50)

SALVATION ARMY
Lower Abbey Street (51). Sunday, 1100 and 1900
South Richmond Street (52), Rathmines. Sunday, 1100

INFORMATION

TOURIST INFORMATION
Dublin Tourism, 14 Upper O'Connell Street, Dublin 1.
Tel. 47733; 51 Dawson Street, Dublin 2. Tel. 47333.
Dublin Tourism is one of eight regional companies set up
by Bord Fáilte, the Irish Tourist Board. Advice and
guidance on all aspects of holidays in Dublin and the
rest of Ireland is given, and brochures, guide books, road
maps and timetables are available.

Hours of opening

O'Connell Street, October-April : 0915 to 1715, week-days, 0915 to 1300 Saturdays. May-September : 0830 to 2000 every day including Sunday

Dawson Street, all year : 0915 to 1730 weekdays only
Bord Fáilte, Baggot Street Bridge, Dublin 2. Tel. 65871
C.I.E. Information, Passenger Trains and Buses. Tel. 47911 weekdays 0900 to 2100, Sundays 1000 to 2100.
C.I.E. Information Booth, centre of O'Connell Street, every day except Sunday 0900 to 2000.

GOVERNMENT INFORMATION

Government Information Bureau. Tel. 67571. Do not expect a direct reply; the G.I.B. acts as a clearing-house for inquiries to the various government departments and normally they will accept an inquiry and telephone the reply.
Government Publications Office, G.P.O. Arcade, off Henry Street, Dublin 1. Tel. 42541. Acts, Parliamentary Bills, White Papers, Maps etc. for sale.

MISCELLANEOUS INFORMATION

Ask the Experts, Evening Press, Burgh Quay, Dublin 2. Such inquiries as the value of a 1933 penny, how to write to Steve McQueen or Racquel Welch, or is my poetry poetry? are all answered expertly though often quite facetiously in this regular newspaper column.
What's on : Cultural and other events for Dublin and elsewhere, listed in the second last page of the *Irish Times*.
Cu Fola : c/o 179 Pearse Street, Dublin 2. The Irish word for blood-hound; specialises in Irish problems of any nature, geological, sociological, topographical etc. It will also execute problems of a more practical nature, such as the location and dispatch of books, newspapers, pictures, etc. Estimates given.

FUTURE INFORMATION (Fortune Tellers) Mrs Sheridan, Tom Clarke House, Ballybough. Mrs O'Brien, Smithfield

Newspapers and Periodicals

Irish Times, mornings, 31 Westmoreland Street, Dublin 2. Tel. 775871

Irish Press, mornings *Evening Press*, evenings *Sunday Press*, Sundays	Irish Press House, O'Connell Street, Dublin 1, tel. 41871. Editorial and Circulation: Burgh Quay, Dublin 2, tel. 757931

Irish Independent *Evening Herald* *Sunday Independent*	Independent Newspapers Ltd, 90 Middle Abbey Street, Dublin 1, tel. 46841

Hibernia Fortnightly Review, 179 Pearse Street, Dublin 2. Tel. 776317
   Politics, current affairs, literature, arts and finance. Fortnightly

This Week, Creation House, Botanic Road, Dublin 9. Tel. 303511
   National and international current affairs. Weekly

Business and Finance, Creation House, Botanic Road, Dublin 9. Tel. 303511
   Irish business news and features. Weekly

United Irishman, 30 Gardiner Place, Dublin 1. Tel. 41045
   Politics and current affairs; official organ of Sinn Féin. Monthly

Irish Field, 31 Westmoreland Street, Dublin 2. Tel. 775871
   Racing paper. Weekly

Irish Tatler and Sketch, 30 Molesworth Street, Dublin 2. Tel. 67291
   Social news. Monthly

Social and Personal, 29/30 Fleet Street, Dublin 2. Tel. 770348/778491
   Society news. Monthly

Young Citizen, Institute of Public Administration, 59 Lansdowne Road, Dublin 4. Tel. 685141
   Monthly during the school year.

Radio Telefís Éireann. Administration and Television Studios : Donnybrook, Dublin 4. Tel. 693111. Telex 5268 *Sound Broadcasting*: Henry Street, Dublin 1. Tel. 42981. *Radio Transmissions* 240m and VHF 95.3 MHz. The domestic current used in Ireland is A.C. 220 volts (single phase) and 380 volts (three phase).

CUSTOMS REGULATIONS

YOU are allowed to bring into the country the following items free of duty :

Spirits—1 bottle ($\frac{1}{6}$ gallon)

Wine—1 bottle ($\frac{1}{6}$ gallon)

Tobacco Goods—400 cigarettes or any assortment of tobacco goods not exceeding 1 lb in weight

Toilet water or perfume—$\frac{1}{2}$ pint

Other articles—£5.00 worth

Articles **liable to duty** include : china, clocks, clothes, confectionery, electrical goods, food, glassware, jewellery, leather goods, motor cars and cycles, musical instruments, razors, sports equipment and toys.

Among the **prohibited** goods are : arms, ammunition, birds, butter, cats, contraceptives, dogs, explosives, fireworks, lottery advertisements, narcotics, plants, plumage (except of course plumage forming part of the passenger's apparel), poultry, and indecent or obscene books or pictures.

Passports : Passport Office, 39 Dawson Street, Dublin 2. Tel. 780822. Open from 0930 to 1630 Monday to Friday.

CULTURAL CONTACTS

The Arts Council, 70 Merrion Square, Dublin 2. Tel. 62615

An Taisce, The National Trust, Bridge House, 126 Baggot Street, Dublin 2. Tel. 64023

P.E.N. Club, Hon. Secretary, Mr. Desmond Clarke, R.D.S., Ballsbridge, Dublin 4. Tel. 680645

Musical Association of Ireland, 11 Suffolk Street, Dublin 2. Tel. 770976

Comhaltas Ceoltoiri Éireann (Irish Musicians' Association) 6 Harcourt Street, Dublin 2. Tel. 757554

Conradh na Gaeilge (Gaelic League), 6 Harcourt Street, Dublin 2. Tel. 757401

Dublin Grand Opera Society, 11a South Leinster Street, Dublin 2. Tel. 771717

Dublin Institute for Advanced Studies, 9/10 Burlington Road, Dublin 4. Tel 680748

Irish Film Society, 12 Merrion Square, Dublin 2. Tel. 66213

National Film Institute of Ireland, 65 Harcourt Street, Dublin 2. Tel. 753638

Royal Dublin Society, Ballsbridge, Dublin 4. Tel. 680645

Royal Irish Academy, 19 Dawson Street, Dublin 2. Tel. 62570

Royal Irish Academy of Music, 36 Westland Row, Dublin 2. Tel. 66843

Irish Folklore Commission, 82 St Stephen's Green, Dublin 2. Tel. 752440

Irish Georgian Society, 50 Mountjoy Square, Dublin 1. Tel. 41494

Irish Book Publishers' Association, 179 Pearse Street, Dublin 2. Tel 779738

BUSINESS CONTACTS

Dublin Chamber of Commerce, 7 Clare Street, Dublin 2. Tel. 64291

Dublin Junior Chamber of Commerce, 7 Clare Street, Dublin 2. Tel. 64291

Federated Union of Employers, 8 Fitzwilliam Place, Dublin 2. Tel. 65126

Córas Tráchtála (C.T.T.—Irish Export Board), Lansdowne Road, Ballsbridge, Dublin 4. Tel. 65881

Confederation of Irish Industry, 28 Fitzwilliam Place, Dublin 2. Tel. 60366

National Development Association, 3 St Stephen's Green, Dublin 2. Tel. 777305

Industrial Development Authority, Lansdowne House, Ballsbridge, Dublin 4. Tel. 685161

Department of Industry and Commerce, Kildare Street, Dublin 2. Tel. 65801

Irish Management Institute, 186 Orwell Road, Dublin 14. Tel. 904681

Irish Congress of Trade Unions, 19 Raglan Road, Dublin 4. Tel. 680641

Consumer's Association of Ireland, 35 Wicklow Street, Dublin 2. Tel. 770197

Rotary Club of Ireland, Mr M. L. Mulligan, 'Alverna', Foxrock Park, Dublin. Tel. 894459

Skal Club, Hon. Sec. Mr John Purcell, Bord Fáilte, Baggot Street Bridge. Tel. 65871

Lions Club, President, Mr Tullio, Trimlestown House, Booterstown, Co. Dublin. Tel. 692577

EMBASSIES AND CONSULAR OFFICES

Argentine : Argentine Embassy, 15 Ailesbury Drive, Ballsbridge, Dublin 4. Tel. 691546

Australia : Australian Embassy, 6th Floor, Fitzwilton House, 6 Wilton Terrace, Dublin 2. Tel. 67294

Austria : Austrian Embassy, 5 Ailesbury Road, Ballsbridge, Dublin 4. Tel. 694577

Belgium : Belgian Embassy, Shrewsbury House, Shrewsbury Road, Dublin 4. Tel. 692082

Britain : British Embassy, 39 Merrion Square, Dublin 2. Tel. 65196

Canada : Canadian Embassy, 10 Clyde Road, Ballsbridge, Dublin 4. Tel. 680628

Denmark : Danish Consulate-General, 71 Lower Leeson Street, Dublin 2. Tel. 60880

Finland : Finnish Consulate-General, 19 Lower Pembroke Street, Dublin 2. Tel. 673319

France : French Embassy, 53 Ailesbury Road, Ballsbridge, Dublin 4. Tel. 692071

Germany : German Embassy, 43 Ailesbury Road, Ballsbridge, Dublin 4. Tel. 693011

Holy See : The Apostolic Nunciature, Phoenix Park, Dublin 7. Tel. 771030

Iceland : Icelandic Consulate, 6 Monkstown Avenue, Monkstown, Co. Dublin. Tel. 771030

India : Indian Embassy, 58 Upper Leeson Street, Dublin 2. Tel. 67131

Italy : Italian Embassy, 12 Fitzwilliam Square, Dublin 2. Tel. 62401

Japan : Japanese Embassy Office, 22 Ailesbury Road, Ballsbridge, Dublin 4. Tel. 684609

Mexico : Mexican Consulate, 17 Lower Baggot Street, Dublin 2. Tel. 62745

Malta : Honorary Consul, Mr Noel Judd, 1 Upper Fitz-william Street, Dublin 2. Tel. 60331

Monaco : Consulate-General, 30 Lansdowne Road, Balls-bridge, Dublin 4. Tel. 63362

Netherlands : Netherlands Embassy, 160 Merrion Road, Dublin 4. Tel. 693444

Nigeria : Nigerian Embassy, 15 Ailesbury Road, Balls-bridge, Dublin 4. Tel. 692555

Norway : Norwegian Consulate, 17 College Green, Dublin 2. Tel. 777635

Portugal : Portuguese Embassy, 14 Ailesbury Road, Ballsbridge, Dublin 4. Tel. 692512

Spain : Spanish Embassy, Ailesbury House, Ailesbury Road, Ballsbridge, Dublin 4. Tel. 691640

Sweden : Swedish Embassy, 31 Merrion Road, Dublin 4. Tel. 694544

Switzerland : Swiss Embassy, 6 Ailesbury Road, Dublin 4. Tel. 692515

Turkey : Turkish Consulate, 122 St Stephen's Green, Dublin 2. Tel. 758721

U.S.A : American Embassy and Consulate-General, 42 Elgin Road, Ballsbridge, Dublin 4. Tel. 64061

IRISH/ENGLISH GLOSSARY

FEW (if any) people in Dublin speak Irish exclusively, but certain Irish words are frequently used, mainly in a topographical or political context, and the following list may be of some help.

POLITICAL AND OFFICIAL EXPRESSIONS

An t-Oireachtas Oireachtas literally means assembly; the term is used in the Constitution to denote the whole system of Government

An Uachtarán   the President

An Dáil   the Lower House of the Oireachtas, equivalent to the British House of Commons

An Seanad   the Senate, or Upper House of the Oireachtas

An Teachta Dála   usually abbreviated to T.D., a member of the Dáil

Teach Laighean   Leinster House, where the Dáil and Senate meet

An Rialtas   the Government

An Taoiseach   literally 'the Chief', the Prime Minister

An Tánaiste   literally 'next in order', the deputy Prime Minister

An Aire   the Minister; thus 'An Aire Cosanta', the Minister for Defence

An Státseirbhís   the Civil Service

An Roinn   The Department, thus An Roinn Cosanta, the Department of Defence

Bunreacht na hÉireann   The Constitution of Ireland

TOPOGRAPHICAL EXPRESSIONS

Éire   Ireland

Baile Átha Cliath   Dublin

Sráid   street, as in Sráid Uí Chonaill—O'Connell Street

Bóthar   road

An Lár   the city centre

MISCELLANEOUS EXPRESSIONS

Oifig an Phoist   post office

Córas Iompair Éireann   usually abbreviated to C.I.E., it means Transport Organisation of Ireland

Bord Fáilte   the Irish Tourist Board

Fir   men (usually used to denote men's lavatories)

Mná   women (usually used to denote ladies' lavatories)

142

N

Kilshane
Dubber
Cappagh
Jamestown

Finglas
Wadelai
Ballygall
Cremore

11

Santry
Beaumont
Whitehall
Griffith Ave.
Glasnevin
Drumcondra

9

Coolock
Artane
Harmonstown
Killester

5

Arbour Hill
Smithfield
Fourcourts

Grangegorman
Phibsborough

Cabra
Oxmantown

7

Clonliffe
Dollymount
Ballybough

3

Fairview
Clontarf
Marino
East Wall

Islandbridge
Inchicore
Kilmainham
Merchant's Quay

8

1

10

Ballyfermot

The Coombe
Dolphin's Barn
South Circular Rd.
Portobello

2

South Quays
Pearse Street
Westmoreland Street
College Green
Dame Street
Dublin Castle
Lord Edward Street
Sth. Gt. George's Street
Camden Street
Harcourt Street
St. Stephen's Green
Grafton Street
Nassau Street
Dawson Street
Kildare Street
Merrion Square
Govt. Buildings
Mount Street
Fitzwilliam Square

Bluebell
Drimnagh
Crumlin

Walkinstown
Perrystown

12

Harolds Cross
Ranelagh
Rathmines
Sandford
Dartry
Rathgar
Milltown
Terenure

6

Ringsend
Irishtown
Pembroke
Ballsbridge
Sandymount
Donnybrook
Merrion

4

North Wall
Amiens Street
Talbot Street
Summerhill
Gardiner Street
Mountjoy Sq
Dorset Street
Parnell Street
Capel Street
Abbey Street
Henry Street
O'Connell Street

Dundrum
Goatstown
Ballinteer
Ballyboden
Rockbrook

14

Windy Arbour
Roebuck
Churchtown
Rathfarnham

Bird's Eye Map of Dublin showing Postal Districts

The Essential Map
of Dublin

This street map of Dublin is based on Ordnance Survey by permission of the Government Permit No. 1786.

The plan on the following page shows how the original large street map has been divided into one-page sections and how each section relates to the others.

1	2	3	4	5	6	7	8	9
10	11	12	13	14	15	16	17	
18	19	20	21	22	23	24		
	25	26	27	28	29	30			
	31	32	33	34	35	36	37	38	39
	40	41	42	43	44	45	46	47	48	49

Map Reference

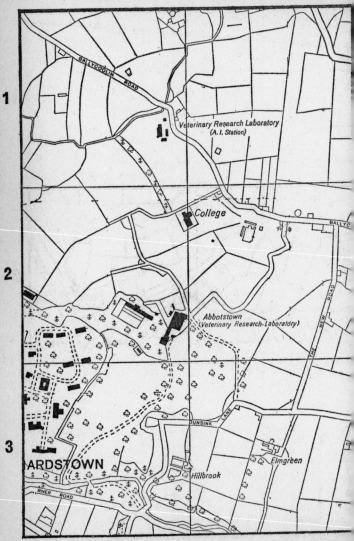

A

B

1

BALLYCOOLIN ROAD

Veterinary Research Laboratory
(A. I. Station)

College

BALLYC

2

Abbotstown
(Veterinary Research Laboratory)

THE NEW ROAD

3

DUNSINK LANE

Elmgreen

ARDSTOWN

Hillbrook

RIVER ROAD

1

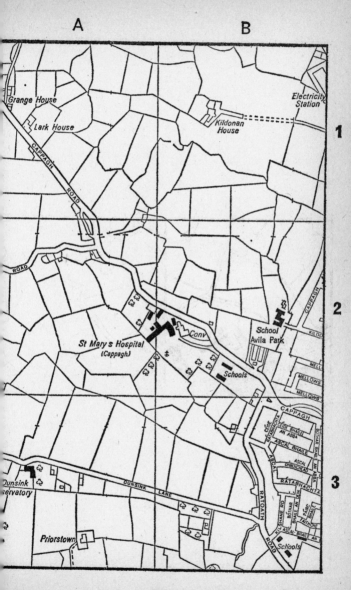

A   B

Grange House

Lark House

Electricity
Station

Kildonan
House

1

CAPPAGH

ROAD

ROAD

St Mary's Hospital
(Cappagh)

Conv

School
Avila Park

2

Schools

MELLOWS

MELLOWS

MELLOWS

CAPPAGH

CÓS
BÁTAIBHTOTH

CÉIDE BHAILE
AN ABÁ

BÓTHAR

ASCAL BHAILE

ASCAL
ÓHÓICHEAD

Dunsink
Observatory

DUNSINK   LANE

ASCAL

RÁTABHACHTA

3

RATOATH

Priorstown

BÓTHAR
AN DÚIN

ASCAL BHAILE
AN

ASCAL BHAILE
AN
FAITHCHE

ROAD

Schools

2

A   B

To St Margaret's

1

NORTH ROAD

MARGARET'S ROAD

ST MARGARET'S ROAD

Mc KELVEY AVE
McKELVEY RD

OAKWOOD ROAD

SYCAMORE
OAKW
OAK

PLUNKETT CRESCENT
PLUNKETT AVENUE

SYCAMORE ROAD

2

PLUNKETT
PLUNKETT
GR
BARRY
Sch
BARRY
AVENUE
BARRY
PARK
Sch
CASEMENT
CASEMENT GR
CASEMENT
CASEMENT
AVE
PARK
CASEMENT ROAD
GLINN DRIVE
GLINN ROAD
KILDONAN ROAD
KILDONAN AVE
KILDONAN
KILDONAN AVE
FINGLASWOOD ROAD
CARDIFF CASTLE RD

CLANCY AVE
CLANCY AVE
CLANCY ROAD

MCKEE ROAD

GROVE AVE

OAKWOOD ROAD
BALLYGALL

FINGLAS
BALLYGALL AVE

WS PARK
WS PARK
AVENUE
ROAD
ROAD

MELLOWS ROAD
CAPPAGH DR

FINGLAS

JAMESTOWN ROAD
NORTH ROAD
MCKEE AVENUE

Clinic

BALLYGALL ROAD W

CLUNE RD

COLLINS AVE
COLLINS GREEN
GLASAREE RD
Sch
Scho

3

AN ABBA
ARDUIBH I

Schools
Schools
CHURCHFIELD
CHURCHFIELD RD
School
Conv
Conv
Schs
ASCAL AIRD AN TOBAIR
CLUÁN RD
CÉIDE
AIRD AN TOBAIR
HAILE AN DÉIN
BOTHAR AIRD AN TOBAIR
ASCAL DHÚN SINCE
FÁITHCHE DHÚN SINCE
GAIRDÍN DHÚN SINCE
PÁIRC DHÚN SINCE
BOTHAR DHÚN SINCE
THE LAWN
CHURCH
MAIN STREET
Schs
Conv
Conv
BALLYGALL ROAD W
COLLINS
BALLYGALL GR
BALLYGALL ROAD
SYCAMORE ROAD
BALLYGALL PARADE
BALLYGALL CRESCENT

Sports
Grounds

St Helena

FINGLAS ROAD

Football
Grounds

3

School

Priorswood
House

CLONSAUGH ROAD

1

RIVERSIDE PARK
RIVERSIDE GROVE
RIVERSIDE DRIVE
GREENCASTLE DRIVE
GLIN DRIVE
GLIN AVE
GLIN ROAD
KILGROM
RIVERSIDE CRES
GREENCASTLE ROAD
RIVERSIDE ROAD

Larch Hill

Brook House

Kilmore
House

KILMORE

OSCAR TRAYNOR ROAD

School

Subway

BARRYSCOURT
ADARE AVE
ADARE GREEN
ADARE ROAD
ADARE DRIVE
DUNRALLY ROAD
Sch

CASTLETIMON ROAD
CASTLETIMON PARK
CASTLETIMON AVE
CASTLETIMON GREEN

CONSAUGH ROAD

KILBARRON DR
KILBARRON AVE
KILBARRON PARK

CROMCASTLE GN
CROMCASTLE AVE
CROMCASTLE PK
CROMCASTLE ROAD

1

BALLYSHANNON
ROAD

Schs

KILBARRON ROAD

CROMCASTLE DR

KILMORE ROAD

KILMORE AVENUE
KILMORE CRES
COOLOCK AVENUE
COOLOCK DRIVE
COOLOCK GROVE

2

MORGAN
LLAS

CASTLEKEVIN RD

Sch

KILMORE CLOSE

KILMORE DRIVE

Convent

alescent
ome

BEAUMONT

MONTROSE DR
MONTROSE
CRESCENT

HAZELWOOD

Col

COOLGREENA ROAD

ARDMORE GROVE
ARDMORE DRIVE
ARDMORE CLOSE
ARDMORE CRESCENT
ARDMORE PARK

Sch

HAZELWOOD
DRIVE

Sch

CHANEL

Schools

ARDMORE DRIVE

ARDLEA ROAD
CHANEL AVE
ARDBEG
ARDBEG

MARYFIELD

3

BEAUMONT ROAD

SKELLY'S LANE

CRESCENT
MAYBERY
KILMORE ROAD
ARDCOLLUM AVE
ROAD
DANIEL

3

COOLATREE RD

ELM MOUNT PARK

LING ROAD

6

ELM MOUNT ROAD

2

School

1

Newgrove Ho.

Woodlawns

The Grange

Grangemore

The Donahies

THE RISE

DONAGHMEDE ROAD

2

TONLEGEE ROAD

KILBARRACK ROAD

Station

Kilbarrack Road Estate

WOODBINE ROAD

WOODBINE CLO

WOODBINE DR.

GRANGE ROAD

Sch

PARK PARADE

Sch

Sta.

GROVE

BRIARFIELD

THORNVILLE AVE.

GRANGE PARK GROVE

GRANGE PARK AVENUE

GRANGE PK. WALK

GRANGE PK. CLOSE

GRANGE PARK RISE

GRANGE PK. GREEN

BRIARFIELD ROAD

ROSE GLEN AVE.

THORNVILLE RD.

KILBARRACK GROVE

GRANGE PARK ROAD

Sch

Blackbanks Estate

Hostel

ROSE GLEN ROAD

3

Walmer

FOXFIELD GROVE

Sports Grounds

QUAY WK.

FOXFIELD AVENUE

FOXFIELD PARK

FOXFIELD ROAD

ST. ASSAM'S PARK

RATHMORE PARK

ST. ASSAM'S RD. W.

ST. ASSAM'S AVENUE

HOWTH ROAD

ta.

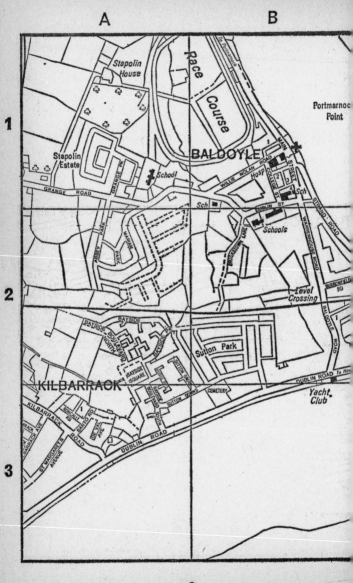

A B

Football
Grounds

HAWTHORN LAWN

BEECH PARK AVE

Sch

TLEKNOCK

School

The Farm

COLLEGE ROAD

College

Mount
Hybla

Farmleigh

maroon
ouse

ER LIFFEY

terstown

Schools

Convent

Ashtown
Lodge

Schools

PECK'S LANE

Park Villas

Phœnix Park
Race Course

Ash

DEERPARK ROAD

DEERPARK AVE

DEERPARK DRIVE

Castleknock

Cas
Par

WHITE'S ROAD

White's Gate

Ordnance Survey
Office

Tink

1

2

3

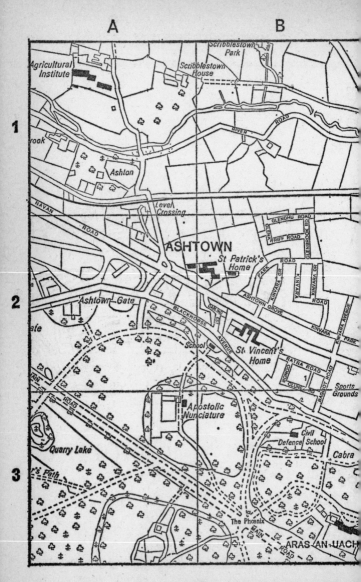

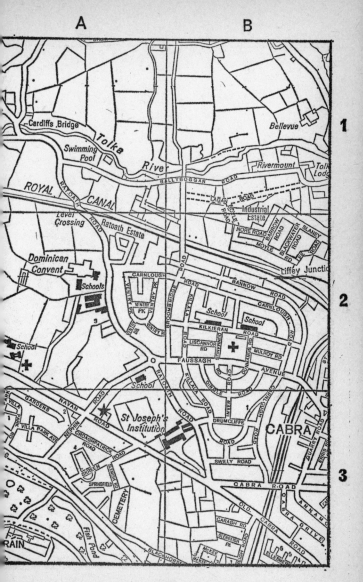

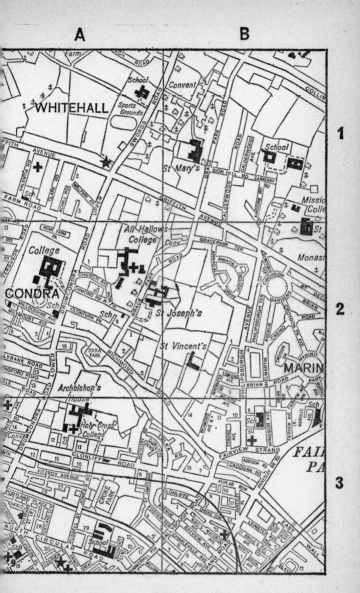

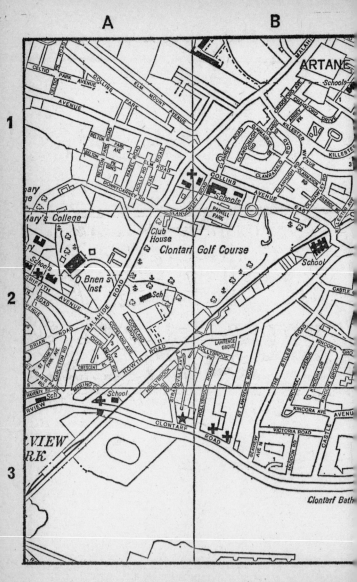

RAHENY

FOX'S LANE

D

MAIN ST

AVONDALE

MAYWOOD AVENUE

PARK

MAYWOOD

RD

GODDAMH

JAMES LARKIN ROAD

Convent

RAHENY PK

MAYWOOD

DR

MAYWOOD GR

MAYWOOD LN

School

ÁIT MHÚILINN ASCAL AN MHÚILINN

WATERMILL

FAIRR-AN MHÚILINN

ASCAL AN MHÚILINN

ROAD

ARDAN ÁINE

NAOMH ÁINE

1

NAOMH

Bettyglen

Football   Grounds

St Anne's
(in Ruins)

BULL

AVENUE

PARK

2

MOUNT

Manresa
Retreat Ho

NORTH

Royal Dublin Golf Links

UNT

3

Bull Wall
Cottages

BULL.

Club House

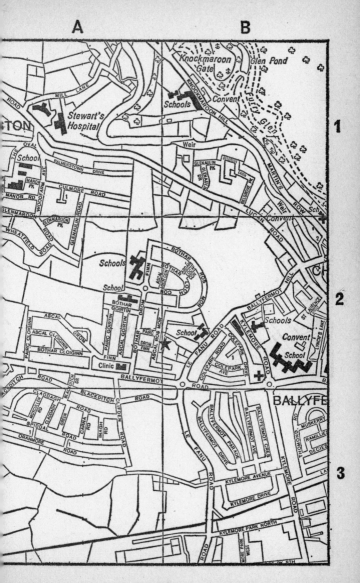

A   B

1

2

3

Knockmaroon Gate

Glen Pond

Tully Glen

Convent

KNOCKMAROON HILL

Schools

Stewart's Hospital

MILL LANE

...TON

ROAD

THE OVAL

School

PALMERSTOWN DRIVE

MANOR PK.

WOODFARM AVE.

MANOR RD.

CULMORE ROAD

GLENMAROON

GLENMAROON PK.

GLENAULIN ROAD

WHEATFIELD ROAD

Weir

GLENAULIN PK.

GLENAULIN DR.

BELGROVE PK.

MARTIN'S ROW

Weir

Sch.

LUCAN ROAD

Convent

Schools

BÓTHAR FINN

BÓTHAR ROS

ASCAL DROM

ASCAL ROS

BÓTHAR CLOIGINN

School

BÓTHAR GOIRTIN

ASCAL GOIRTIN

PAIRC GOIRTIN

PAIRC FINN

DROM FINN

School

LE FANU ROAD

BALLYFERMOT ROAD

Schools

KYLEMORE ROAD

Convent

School

LYNCH'S LANE

ASCAL CLOIGINN

PAIRC CLOIGINN

BÓTHAR CLOIGINN

Clinic

ASCAL FINN

COLEPARK ROAD

COLEPARK DRIVE

COLEPARK AVE.

BALLYFERMOT ROAD

BLACKDITCH ROAD

CLODAGH RD.

MOYGLARE RD.

CLODAGH GREEN

CARNA RD.

INAGH RD.

BLACKDITCH ROAD

CLIFDEN ROAD

BALLYFE...

BALLYFERMOT DRIVE

BALLYFERMOT PARADE

BALLYFERMOT AVE.

BALLYFERMOT CRES.

MUSKERRY RD.

RAMILLIES RD.

DECIES RD.

DRUMFINN RD.

SPIDDAL RD.

ORANMORE ROAD

ROAD

LE FANU ROAD

KYLEMORE AVENUE

KYLEMORE ROAD

KYLEMORE DRIVE

KYLEMORE PARK NORTH

KYLEMORE PARK

18

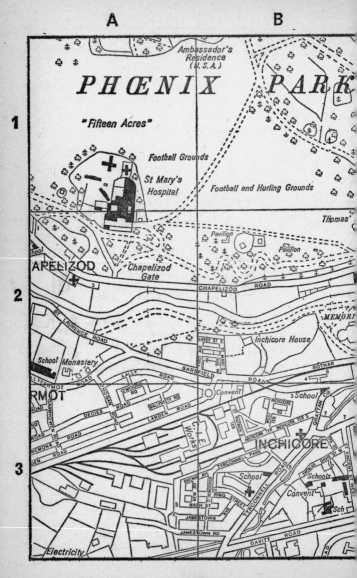

A   B

1

PHŒNIX   *PARK*

Ambassador's Residence (U.S.A.)

"Fifteen Acres"

Football Grounds

St Mary's Hospital

Football and Hurling Grounds

Thomas'

Pavilion

Pavilion

APELIZOD

Chapelizod Gate

CHAPELIZOD ROAD

2

ST LAURENCE ROAD

MEMORI

Inchicore House

School   Monastery

LIFFEY ST S

OILL AVE

AVE W

SARSFIELD

BOTHAR

LLYFERMOT

LALLY ROAD

ROAD

LALLY ROAD

O'MOORE RD

Convent

INCHICORE SQ

School

RMOT

DECIES ROAD

CHOGAN ROAD

GARROW ROAD

BALLYBETTY RD

LANDEN ROAD

PATRICKS

TER

INCHICORE PARK

WEST

ABERCORN TER

INCHICORE TER S

GRATTAN CR

School

SEMONA ROAD

ROAD

AERCORN ROAD

G.S.R. Works

INCHICORE

3

DEN ROAD

RAILWAY AVE

AD AVE NW

MOORE AVE

RING STREET

School

TYRCONNELL PARK

TYRCONNELL ROAD

THOMAS DAVIS ST S

Schools

VINCENT ST WES

NASH ST

Convent

Sch

JAMESTOWN ST

JAMESTOWN RD

TYRCONNELL AVE

DAVITT ROAD

Electricity

19

A   **B**

Abattoir

McKEE BARRACKS   AVENUE   OLD

Cattle Market

Polo Ground

MARLBOROUGH

ZOOLOGICAL GARDENS

OXMANTOWN

Garda Síochána H. Qrs.

NORTH CIRCULAR   ROAD

AUGHRIM

Athletic Ground

O'DEVANEY GDNS.

Hosp.

1

Cricket Gd

The Hollow

INFIRMARY

Citadel Pond

Cricket Gd

PEOPLES' GARDEN

ST. BRICIN'S PK.

Army Athletic Ground

MAIN

Dept. of Defence

MONTPELIER HILL

Wellington Monument

ROAD

Islandbridge Gate

CONYNGHAM   ROAD

PARKGATE ST.

ISLANDBRIDGE

WOLF

VIC

Heuston Sta.

KINGSBRIDGE

Weir

CLANCY BKS.

Hospital

2

STEEVENS LANE

PARK

Hurling Grounds

SOUTH

St. JOHN'S ROAD WEST

Hospital

St

MILITARY ROAD

BOW LANE W.

Royal Hospital (Disused)

BOW BRIDGE

JAMES'S

BEARD

CIRCULAR

13   ST. LR.   23

CHAPELIZOD

17

KILMAINHAM LANE

MOUNT BROWN

Sch

ROAD

Museum

ROAD

OLD

KILMAINHAM

Conv

Sch

EMMET

School

BULFIN GDNS.

KILMAINHAM

Hospitals

BROOKFIELD RD.

BULFIN

ROAD

SOUTH

CONNOLLY

INNER RD.

Conv

MOUNTSHANNON RD.

3

RICHMOND

SUIR

11   12

CIRCULAR

GRAND CANAL BANK

GOLDENBRIDGE

STEPHENS RD.

ROAD

NEW IRELAND RD.

FIFTH

ST. ANTHONY'S RD.

REUBEN

AVENUE

DEVOY

ROAD

PROGRESS RD.

ROAD

DAVITT

ROAD

NEW IRELAND RD.

HERBERTON

REUBEN

BENMADIGAN

GALTYMORE DR.

GALTYMORE

SLIEVENAMON

ROAD

DOLPHIN

School

ROAD

DOLPHIN'S BARN

BEN EDLIN

ROAD

MOURNE

ROAD

20

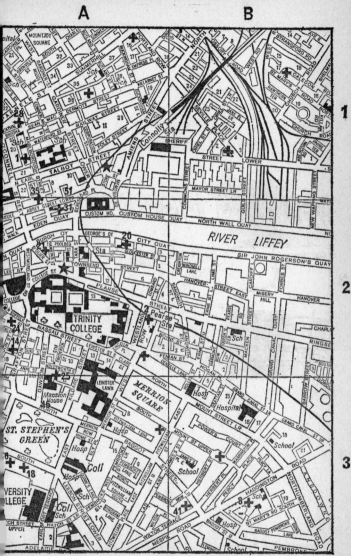

A **B**

1

2

3

School

BARGY RD

RAVENSDALE RD

EAST WALL RD

MERCHANTS RD

BOND ROAD

TOLKA QUAY

TOLKA

ALEXANDRA ROAD.

ERIFF STREET UPPER

EAST WALL ROAD

ALEXANDRA QUAY

CASTLEFORBES UPPER

ALEXANDRA BASIN

TH WALL QUAY

Ferry

Lighthouse.

BENSON ST

GREEN ST E

BRITAIN ST

YORK ROAD

Schs

RINGSEND PARK

PIGEON HOUSE

QUAY

THORNCASTLE STREET

IVEAGH

CAMBRIDGE ROAD

RINGSEND

TE QUAY

ROAD

Greyhound Race Track

BRIDGE ST

FITZWILLIAM ST

RINGSEND PARK

Sports Grounds

OCK ST

RIVOLI

IRISHTOWN

STRAND

PLUNKETT AV

IRISHTOWN

South

11 12

Bath

10

Ch

Church AV

BATH AVENUE

O'CONNELL GARDENS

LONDONBRIDGE RD

CRANFIELD

10

11

BEACH ROAD

14

Hockey Gd

13

34

Sch

LAMB'S TER

BEACH AV

SEAFORT AV

Lansdowne Rugby Gd

NEWBRIDGE AVE

TRITONVILLE ROAD

SANDYMOUNT ROAD

MARINE DR

SEAPORT AV

BEACH

SHELBOURNE ROAD

LANSDOWNE ROAD

HERBERT RD

HERBERTVILLE RD

PARK

CLAREMONT

37

Sch

Conv

L.C. Sta

SERPENTINE

23

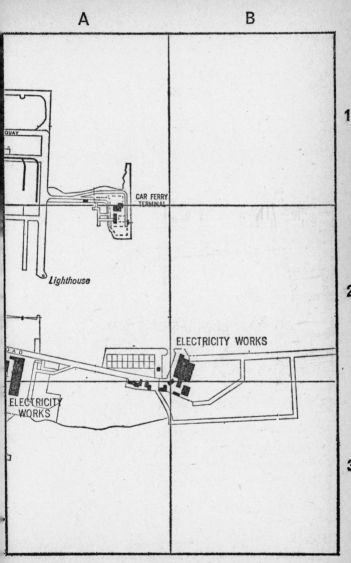

QUAY

CAR FERRY
TERMINAL

Lighthouse

ROAD

ELECTRICITY WORKS

ELECTRICITY
WORKS

A

B

1

2

3

24

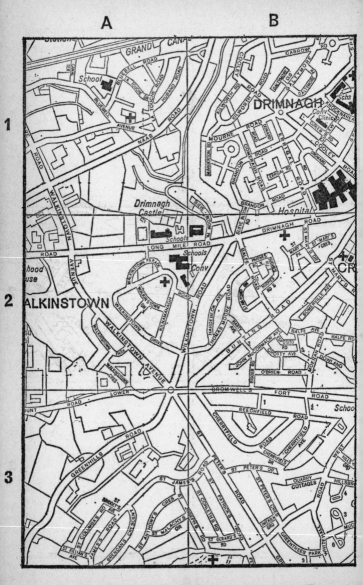

A
B

1

GRAND CANAL

School

BLUEBELL ROAD

LA TOUCHE DRIVE

HUBAND ROAD

AVENUE

BLUEBELL

ROAD

NAAS

WALKINSTOWN

ROAD

CARROW

KILWORTH ROAD

COOLEY ROAD

GALTYMORE

OASTRIOGE

DRIMNAGH

Conv

Clinics

MOURNE

MANGERTON RD

BRANDON

SLIEVE BLOOM ROAD

CONGREVE ROAD

ERRIGAL RD

COOLEY

DOWLAND

BRANDON ROAD

BRANDON ROAD

Hospital

KNOCKNAREA

Schs

Drimnagh
Castle

SLIEVE BLOOM RD

Schools

DRIMNAGH ROAD

ROAD

LONG MILE ROAD

Schools

St
MARY'S
PK

St. MARY'S
CRES.

ROAD

2

ALKINSTOWN

AVENUE

Conv

WALKINSTOWN PARADE

WALKINSTOWN DRIVE

KILNAMANAGH RD

WALKINSTOWN PARK

WALKINSTOWN

WILLINGTON

ROAD

HALDEBECK AVE

THOMAS MOORE ROAD

MARY

RD

BURTING

ROAD

HUGHES

RD

St. MARY'S AVE

BROMFIELD AVE

CR

St. MARY'S

hood
use

ROAD

AVENUE

WALKINSTOWN

CRES

WALKINSTOWN AVENUE

WALKINSTOWN

JOHN Mc CORMACK AV

OSSIO
RD

CROTTY AV

O'BRIEN ROAD

BIGGER RD

MORGAN ROAD

BALFE AVE

BALFE RD

DOWLAND

3

LOWER

GREENHILLS

ROAD

ROAD

CROMWELL'S

BEECHFIELD

FORT

ROAD

ROAD

School

CHERRYFIELD

ROAD

CHERRYFIELD AVE

DR

CHERRYFIELD

St JAMES'S ROAD

St PETER'S

St PETER'S DR

St PATRICK'S ROAD

St COLUMB'S RD

ROAD

QUARRY
COTTAGES

WEST
HILLS GRD

HILLSBR

ST BRIGID'S AVE

St COLUMB'S ROAD

JAMES'S RD

BRENDAN'S CRESCENT

St ANTHONY'S RD

St MALACHY'S DR

St GERARD'S RD

St CONLETH'S RD

GREENHILLS PARK

WHITE HALL

St KILIAN'S AVE

25

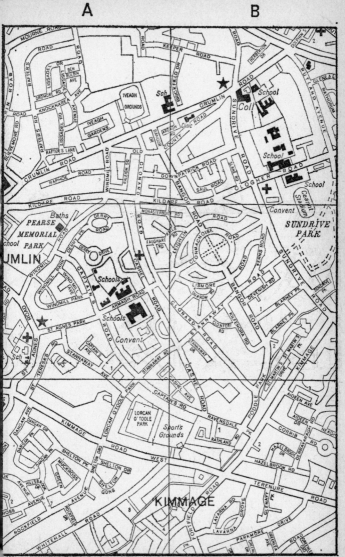

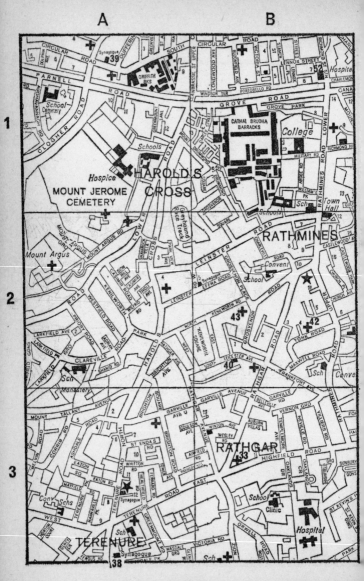

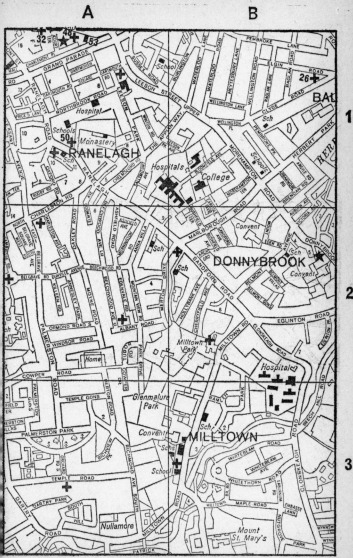

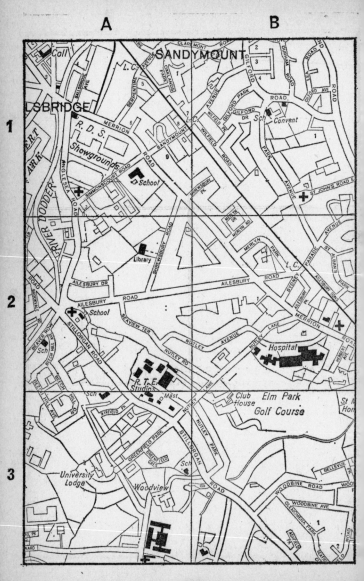

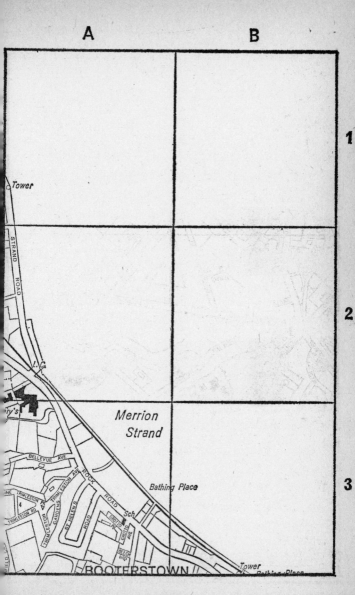

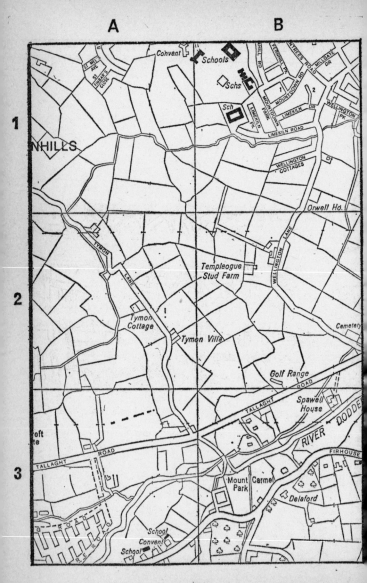

A   **B**

Convent   Schools

Schs

St. Mills Ave.
St. Linbars Close

ST MILLS AVE

Sch

FERNHILL RD
FERNHILL PK
N'TREE'S ROAD
MILLGATE DR

MOUNTDOWN RD

MOUNTDOWN PARK
LIMEKILN DR

MOUNTDOWN PARK

2

1 NHILLS

LIMEKILN DR

WELLINGTON PK

LIMEKILN ROAD

WELLINGTON
COTTAGES

Orwell Rd.

TYMON LANE

Templeogue
Stud Farm

WELLINGTON LANE

2

Tymon
Cottage

Tymon Villa

Cemetery

Golf Range

TALLAGHT ROAD

Spawell
House

RIVER DODDER

oft
te

croft
te

FIRHOUSE

3 TALLAGHT ROAD

Mount
Park

Carmel

Delaford

E R O A D

G

School
Convent

School

31

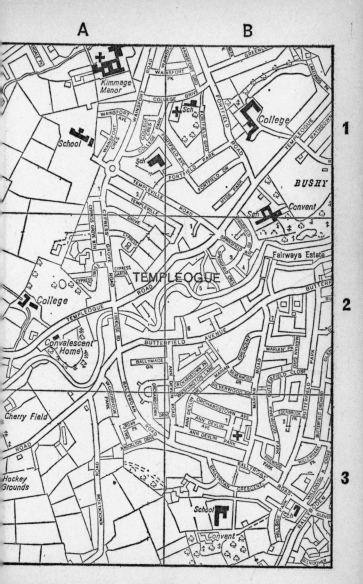

Kimmage Manor

WAINSFORT PK

WAINSFORT ROAD

COLLEGE DRIVE

GREENL

Sch

FORTFIELD GRO

College

TEMPLEOGUE ROAD

RATHDOWN

1

School

WAINSFORT AVE

WAINSFORT CRES

WAINSFORT ROAD

COLLEGE CREST

COLLEGE PARK

FORTFIELD AVE

Sch

FORTFIELD PARK

FORTFIELD GR

FORTFIELD ROAD

HIDE PARK

BUSHY

Sch

Convent

TEMPLEVILLE ROAD

TEMPLEVILLE ROAD

CYPRESS GROVE NTH

CYPRESS GROVE DRIVE

CYPRESS GROVE ROAD

CYPRESS

CYPRESS GARTH

CYPRESS

SPRINGFIELD RD

SPRINGFIELD AVE

SPRINGFIELD CRES

Fairways Estate

TEMPLEOGUE

TEMPLEOGUE ROAD

College

5

BUTTERF

BU

2

Convalescent Home

TEMPLEOGUE ROAD

TIRHOUSE RD

6

BUTTERFIELD AVENUE

CRESCENT

MARIAN PK

MARIAN PARK

GLEN

BALLYMACE GN

ANN DEVLIN ROAD

ORCHARDSTOWN PK

WASHINGTON LANE

ORCHARDSTOWN LANE

MARIAN ROAD

SILVERWOOD DR

SILVERWOOD

MARIAN ROAD

BUTTERFIELD CLOSE

BUTTERFIELD DROMO

BUTTERFIELD PARK

Cherry Field

WOODBROOK

BALLYROAN PARK

ORCHARDSTOWN DRIVE

ANN DEVLIN DRIVE

ORCHARDSTOWN AVE

PINEWOOD CRESCENT

PINEWOOD PARK

EDENBROOK

WILLOWBANK

ROAD

KILMANN

HOGAN PK

ANN DEVLIN AVE

1

ANN DEVLIN PARK

2

WILLOWBANK PK

Hockey Grounds

KNOCKLYON ROAD

KNOCKLYON DRIVE

BALLYROAN CRESCENT

BALLYROAN ROAD

HILLSIDE

PINEWOOD PARK

WILLOWBANK

WILLOWBANK R DRIVE

BALLYBODEN

GLENDA

3

School

Sch

7

Convent

GLENDOHER

33

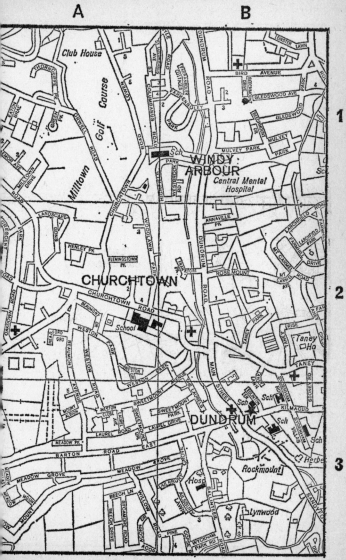

A   B

UNIVERSITY COLLEGE

Roebuck Grove

College

Convent

Convent

Glenard

Roebuck Castle

FOSTERS AVENUE

ST THOMAS ROAD

THE CLOSE

CHESTNUT RD

Convent

ROEBUCK ROAD

THE PINES

MATHER ROAD N

ST COLLEGE RD

MATHER ROAD

LOUVAIN

SALZBURG

CALARY ROAD

WILSON ROAD

NORTH AVENUE

MOUNT MERRION

DEERPARK ROAD

GOATSTOWN ROAD

WILLOWFIELD

ADAM'S ROAD

HOLLYWOOD DR

Mount Anville House

AYLESBURY

ANVILLE

GLENABBEY ROAD

MOUNT TREES ROAD

REDESDALE ROAD

HILL PARK

FARMHILL

TANEY GROVE

Convent

GOATSTOWN

MOUNT

CLONMORE RD

THORNHILL ROAD

ROAD

SILVER BIRCHES

ROAD

KNOCKNASHEE

GLEN PARK

EDEN PARK

School

School

ROAD

KILMACUD

KILMAC

Fairfield

EDEN PARK RD

GLEN PARK AVE

DRUMMARTIN RD

DRUMMARTIN PARK

WOODLEY PARK

SWEETBRIAR LANE

SLIEVE RUA DR

RATHORE AVE

DALE

AVENUE

ANNVILLE DR

KILMAC

School

HILL

Rockfield House

Holywell

KILMACUD

Sch

KILMACUD ROAD UPPER

ST KEVIN'S PARK

HAZEL AVE

DALE GDNS

NUTGROVE

College

LAKELANDS

LAKELANDS DR

ROAD

BALALLY

BALALLY RD

DRIVE

Sch

LAKELANDS AVENUE

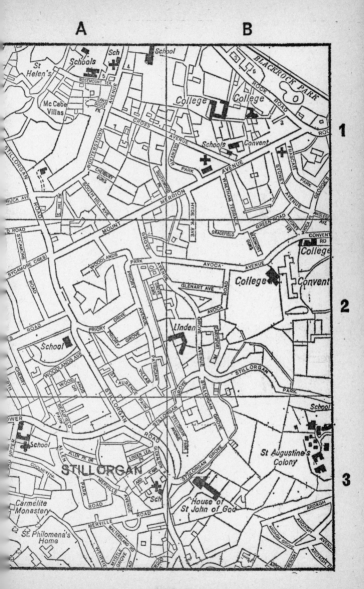

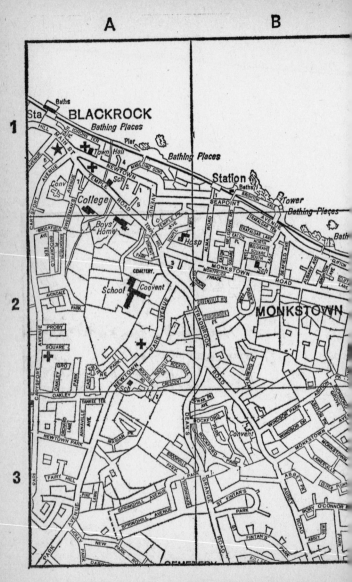

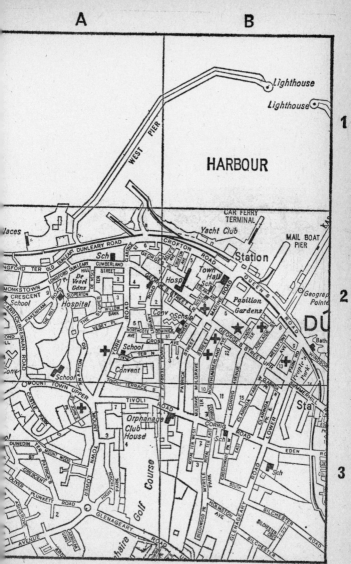

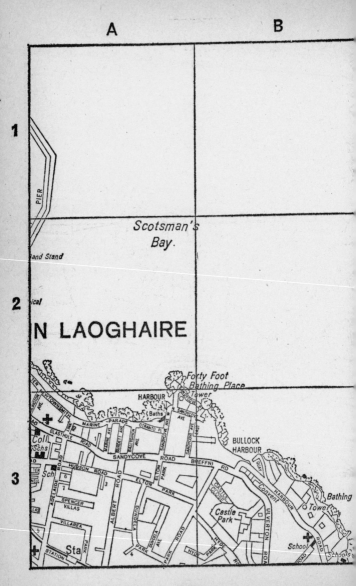

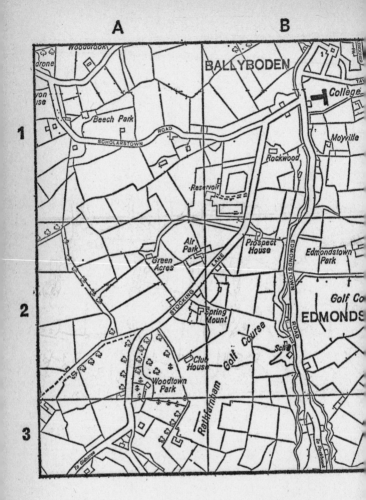

43

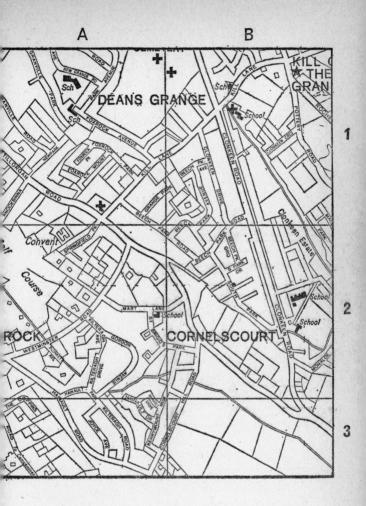

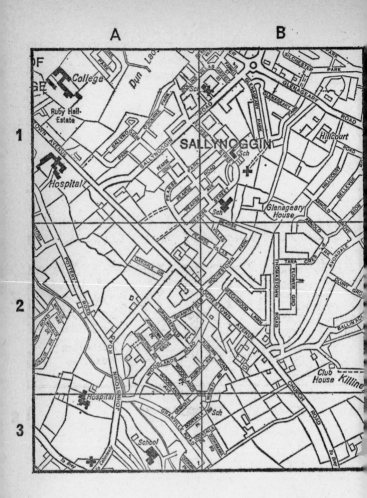

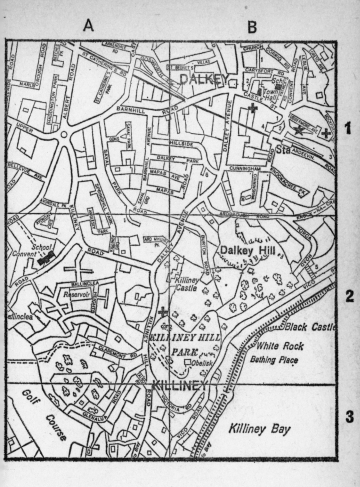

A   B

DALKEY

Town Hall

Sta

1

Dalkey Hill

School
Convent

Killiney
Castle

BALLINCLEA

Reservoir

Black Castle

2

allinclea

KILLINEY HILL

White Rock

PARK

Bathing Place

Obelisk

KILLINEY

Golf

Course

GLENALUA

Killiney Bay

3

48

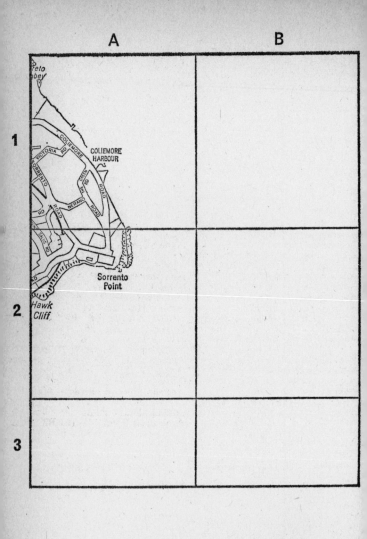

List of Streets

ABBEY PARK (Baldoyle) 9 A2
Abbey Park (Kill of the Grange) 37 B3
Abbey Park (Killester) 15 B1
Abbey Road 37 B3
Abbey Street, Lower 22 A1
Abbey Street, Middle 21 B2 & 22 A2
Abbey Street, Upper 21 B2
Abbey View 37 B3
Abbeyfield 16 A1
Abercorn Road 22 B1
Abercorn Terrace 19 B3
Aberdeen Street 20 B1
Achill Road 14 A1
Acorn Drive 34 A3
Acorn Road 34 A3
Adare Avenue 6 B2
Adare Drive 6 B2
Adare Green 6 B2
Adare Park 6 B2
Adare Road 6 B2
Addison Road 14 B3
Adelaide Road (Leeson Street) 22 A3
Adelaide Road (Dún Laoghaire) 39 A3
Adelaide Street 38 B2
Adrian Avenue 27 A2
Aideen Avenue 26 B3
Aideen Drive 26 B3
Aikenhead Terrace 23 A3
Ailesbury Drive 29 A2
Ailesbury Gardens 29 B2
Ailesbury Grove 34 B3
Ailesbury Lawn 34 B3
Ailesbury Park 29 B2
Ailesbury Road 29 A2-B2
Airfield Park 29 A3
Airfield Road 27 A3-B3
Albany Avenue 37 B2
Albany Road 28 A2
Albert Road 39 A3 & 48 A1
Alexandra Quay 23 A1-B1
Alexandra Road 23 B1
Allen Park Drive 36 A3
Allen Park Road 36 A3
Alma Road 37 B2
Amiens Street 22 A1
Anglesea Avenue 36 B1

Anglesea Road 29 A1-A2
Anglesea Street 21 B2
Anglesey Park 48 A1-A2
Ann Devlin Avenue 32 B3
Ann Devlin Park 32 B3
Ann Devlin Drive 32 B3
Ann Devlin Road 32 B2-B3
Anna Villa 28 A2
Annadale Crescent 14 B2
Annadale Drive 14 B2
Annaly Road 13 A3
Annamoe Drive 13 A3
Annamoe Road 12 B3 & 13 A3
Annamoe Terrace 13 A3
Annaville Avenue 37 A3
Annaville Park 34 B2
Anne Street, South 22 A2
Anner Road 20 A3
Annesley Bridge Road 14 B3
Annesley Park 28 A2
Annesley Place 14 B3
Annville Drive 35 B3
Arbour Hill 21 A1
Ardagh Avenue 36 B3
Ardagh Crescent 36 B3
Ardagh Drive 36 B3
Ardagh Park 36 B3 & 37 A3
Ardagh Road 26 A1-B1
Ardán Loch Con 18 B2
Ardán Naomh Áine 17 A1
Ardbeg Drive 6 B3 & 7 A3
Ardbeg Park 6 B3 & 7 A3
Ardbeg Road 6 B3
Ardbrough Road 48 B1-B2
Ardcollum Avenue 6 B3
Ardee Road 27 B1
Ardee Street 21 A2
Ardeevin Road 48 B1
Ardlea Road 6 B3
Ardmore Close 6 A3
Ardmore Crescent 6 B3
Ardmore Grove 6 A3
Ardmore Park 6 B3
Ardlui Park 45 B1
Ard Mhuire Park 48 A2
Árd-Rí Road 21 A1
Argyle Road 28 B1
Arkendale Road 48 A1
Armagh Road 26 A2
Arnold Grove 47 B1-B2

197

Ballyfermot Avenue 18 B2
Ballyfermot Crescent 18 B3
Ballyfermot Drive 18 B3
Ballyfermot Hill 18 B2
Ballyfermot Parade 18 B3
Ballyfermot Road 18 A2 & 19 A2
Ballygall Avenue 3 B2-B3
Ballygall Crescent 3 B3
Ballygall Parade 3 B3
Ballygall Road 4 A3 & 13 A1
Ballygall Road, West 3 B3
Ballygihen Avenue 39 A3
Ballymace Green 32 A2
Ballymun Avenue 4 A2
Ballymun Drive 4 B3
Ballymun Park 4 A3
Ballymun Road 4 B1 & 13 B1
Ballyneety Road 19 A3
Ballyroan Crescent 32 B3
Ballyroan Park 32 A3
Ballyroan Road 32 A3-B3
Ballyshannon Road 6 A2
Ballytore Road 33 A1-B1
Bangor Drive 26 A1
Bangor Road 26 A1-B2
Bannow Road 12 B2
Bantry Road 14 A1
Bargy Road 23 A1
Barnhill Avenue 48 A1
Barnhill Road 48 A1-B1
Barrow Road 12 B2
Barrow Street 22 B2-B3
Barry Avenue 3 A2
Barry Drive 3 A2
Barry Green 3 A2
Barry Park 3 A2
Barry Road 3 A2
Barryscourt Road 6 B2
Barton Avenue 33 A3
Barton Drive 33 A3
Barton Road, East 34 A3
Barton Road, West 33 A3
Basin Street, Lower 20 B2
Basin Street, Upper 20 B3
Bath Avenue 23 A3
Bath Place 37 A1
Bath Street 23 A3
Baymount Park 16 B2 & 17 A2
Bayside Boulevard, South 9 A3
Bayside Park 9 A2
Bayside Square, East 9 A2
Bayside Square, South 9 A2
Bayside Square, West 9 A2
Bayview Avenue 14 B3

Beach Avenue 23 B3
Beach Drive (Sandymount) 23 B3
Beach Road 23 B3
Beaufield Park 36 A3
Beaumont Avenue 34 A2-A3
Beaumont Drive 14 A2
Beaumont Gardens 36 B2
Beaumont Road 5 B3 & 6 A3
Beaver Row 29 A2
Beech Drive 34 A3
Beeches Park 48 A1
Beechfield Road 25 B3
Beech Grove 30 A3
Beech Hill Avenue 29 A2-A3
Beech Hill Drive 29 A2-A3
Beech Hill Road 28 B2-B3
Beech Park 41 A1
Beech Park Avenue (Blanchardstown) 10 A1
Beech Park Avenue (Deans Grange) 46 B1-B2
Beech Park Drive 46 B2
Beech Park Grove 46 B2
Beech Park Road 46 A1-B2
Beechmount Drive 34 B1
Beechwood Avenue, Lower 28 A2
Beechwood Avenue, Upper 28 A2
Beechwood Lawn 47 B2
Beechwood Park (Dún Laoghaire) 38 B3
Beechwood Road 28 A2
Belcamp Lane 7 A1-B1
Belgrave Avenue 28 A2
Belgrave Road (Rathmines) 28 A2
Belgrave Road (Monkstown) 37 B2
Belgrave Square (Rathmines) 28 A2
Belgrave Square (Monkstown) 37 B2
Belgrove Park 18 B1
Belgrove Road 16 A3
Belleville Avenue 27 B3
Bellevue 21 A2
Bellevue Avenue (Dalkey) 48 A2
Bellevue Avenue (Merrion) 30 A3
Bellevue Park 29 B3
Bellevue Road 47 A1

199

Belmont Avenue 28 B2
Belmont Gardens 28 B2
Belmont Villas 28 B2
Belton Park Avenue 15 A1
Belton Park Gardens 15 A1
Belton Park Road 15 A1
Belvedere Place 14 A3
Ben Edar Road 20 B1 & 21 A1
Benbulbin Avenue 26 A1
Benbulbin Road 20 A3
Benburb Street 21 A1
Benmadigan Road 20 A3
Benson Street 23 A2
Beresford Place 22 A1
Beresford Street 21 B1-B2
Berkeley Road 13 B3
Bigger Road 25 B2
Birch's Lane 35 A2-A3
Bird Avenue 34 B1
Bishop Street 21 B3
Blackbanks Estate 8 B3
Blackditch Drive 18 A2-A3
Blackditch Road 18 A2-A3
Blackglen Road 43 B3 & 44 A3
Blackhall Place 21 A1-A2
Blackhall Street 21 A2
Blackheath Avenue 16 A2
Blackheath Drive 16 A2
Blackheath Gardens 16 A2
Blackheath Grove 16 A2
Blackheath Park 16 A2
Blackhorse Avenue 11 A2 &
   20 B1
Blackpitts 21 A3-B3
Blackrock 37 A1
Blackwater Road 12 B2
Blarney Park 26 B2
Blessington Street 21 B1
Bloomfield Avenue (Donnybrook)
   28 B1
Bloomfield Avenue (Portobello)
   27 B1
Bluebell Avenue 25 A1
Bluebell Road 25 A1
Bolton Street 21 B1
Bond Road 23 A1
Bond Street 21 A3
Bonham Street 21 A2
Booterstown 30 A3
Booterstown Avenue 36 A1
Botanic Avenue 13 B2 & 14 A2
Botanic Road 13 B2
Bóthar Árd an Tobair 3 A3
Bóthar Beannaoibhinn 4 A3

Bóthar Bhaile an Abba 2 B3
Bóthar Bhaile an Déin 2 B3
Bóthar Bhaile Harmain 7 B3 &
   16 B1
Bóthar Bhaile Muire 16 B1
Bóthar Cloiginn 18 A2
Bóthar Coilbeard 19 B2 &
   20 A2
Bóthar Dhúin Since 3 A3
Bóthar Dhroichead Chiarduibh
   3 A3
Bóthar Drom Finn 18 A2
Bóthar Goirtín 18 A2
Bóthar Léin 7 B3
Bóthar Loch Con 18 B2
Bóthar Mac Amhlaoi 7 A3
Bóthar Measc 7 A3
Bóthar Mobhi 13 B1-B2
Bóthar na Naomh 16 B1 &
   17 A1
Bóthar Raithean 4 A3
Bóthar Ríbh 7 A3 & 16 B1
Bóthar Ros Mór 18 B2
Bow Bridge 20 B2
Bow Lane, West 20 B2
Boyne Street 22 A2-B2
Braemor Avenue 34 A1
Braemor Drive 33 B1
Braemor Park 33 B1
Braemor Road 33 B1 & 34 A1
Brandon Road 25 B1
Breffni Road 39 B3
Bregia Road 13 A3
Brendan Road 28 B1
Brewery Road 45 A1
Brian Road 14 B2
Brian Terrace 14 B2
Brickfield Drive 26 B1
Bride Road 21 B2
Bride Street 21 B2-B3
Bridge Street, Upper 21 A2
Bridge Street 23 A2
Bridge Street, Lower 21 A2
Brighton Avenue
   (Monkstown) 37 B2
Brighton Avenue
   (Rathgar) 27 A2
Brighton Road
   (Foxrock) 45 B2 & 46 A3
Brighton Road
   (Terenure) 27 A3
Brighton Square 27 A3
Brighton Vale 37 B1

200

201

Clancy Road 3 B2
Clandonagh Road 15 B1
Clanhugh Road 15 B1
Clanmahon Road 15 B1
Clanmaurice Road 15 B1
Clanranald Road 15 B1
Clanree Road 15 B1
Clare Road 14 A1
Clare Street 22 A2
Claremont Drive 4 A3
Claremont Park 23 B3
Claremont Road
 (Killiney) 48 A2
Claremont Road
 (Sandymount) 29 B1
Clarence Mangan Road 21 A3
Clarence Street 38 A2
Clarendon Street 21 B2 &
 22 A2
Clareville Road 27 A2
Clarinda Park, East 38 B3
Clarinda Park, North 38 B2
Clarinda Park, West 38 B3
Claude Road 13 B3
Clifden Road 18 A3
Clifton Avenue 37 B2
Clifton Lane 37 B2
Clifton Terrace 37 B2
Cliftonville Road 13 B2
Clogher Road 26 B1 & 27 A1
Clonard Road 26 A1-B2
Clonfert Road 26 B2
Clonkeen Crescent 46 B1
Clonkeen Drive 46 B1
Clonkeen Estate 46 B1-B2
Clonkeen Road 46 B1-B3
Clonliffe Avenue 14 A3
Clonliffe Gardens 14 A3
Clonliffe Road 14 A3
Clonmacnoise Road 26 B2
Clonmel Road 4 B3
Clonmore Road
 (Goatstown) 35 B2
Clonsaugh Road 6 B1
Clonskeagh Road 28 B2-B3
Clontarf Park 16 A3
Clontarf Road 15 A3 & 16 B3
Clonturk Park 14 A2
Clune Road 3 B2-B3
Cluny Grove 47 B2
Clyde Road 28 B1
Coldwell Street 38 B3 & 39 A3
Colepark Avenue 18 B2
Colepark Drive 18 B2

Colepark Road 18 B2
Coleraine Street 21 B1
Cole's Lane 21 B1
Coliemore Road 49 A1
College Crescent 32 A1
College Drive 32 A1-B1
College Green 22 A2
College Park 32 A1
College Road
 (Castleknock) 10 A2-A3
College Road
 (Whitechurch Road) 42 B2
College Street 22 A2
College Street (Baldoyle) 9 B1
Collins Avenue 14 B1 & 15 B2
Collins Avenue, East 15 B2
Collins Avenue Extension 4
 B3
Collins Green 3 B3
Collins Park 15 A1
Collins Place 3 B3
Comeragh Road 25 B1
Commons Street 22 B1-B2
Connaught Street 13 A3
Connolly Avenue 20 A3
Conor Clune Road 11 B2
Conquer Hill Avenue 16 B3
Conquer Hill Road 16 B3
Constitution Hill 21 B1
Convent Lane 33 A2
Convent Road
 (Blackrock) 38 B2
Convent Road
 (Dalkey) 48 B1
Convent Road
 (Dún Laoghaire) 38 B2
Conyngham Road 20 A2-B2
Cook Street 21 B2
Coolatree Park 5 B3 & 6 A3
Coolatree Road 6 A3
Cooleen Avenue 5 B3
Cooley Road 25 B1
Coolock 7 A3
Coolock Avenue 6 B2
Coolock Close 6 B2
Coolock Drive 7 A2
Coolock Green 6 B2
Coolock Grove 6 B2
Coolrua Drive 5 B3
Copeland Avenue 15 A2
Copeland Grove 15 A2
Cork Street 21 A3
Cornelscourt 46 B2

Deerpark Road 10 B2
Deerpark Road (Mt Merrion) 35 B2
Delville Road 4 B3
Demesne 16 A2
Denmark Street, Great 21 B1
Denmark Street, Little 21 B1
Dermot O'Hurley Avenue 23 A2
Derravaragh Road 26 B3
Derry Drive 26 A2
Derry Park 26 A2
Derry Road 26 A2
Derrynane Gardens 23 A3
De Val Avenue 9 A3
De Vesci Terrace 38 A2
Devenish Road 26 B2
Devoy Road 20 A3
Digges Street, Upper 21 B3
Dingle Road 12 B2-B3
Dispensary Lane 33 A2
Distillery Road 14 A3
Dodder Park Road 33 A1-B1
Dodder Road, Lower 33 A1-B1
D'Olier Street 22 A2
Dollymount 16 B2
Dollymount Avenue 16 B2 & 17 A2
Dollymount Grove 16 B2
Dollymount Park 16 B3
Dolphin Avenue 27 A1
Dolphin Road 20 B3
Dolphin's Barn 20 B3
Dolphin's Barn Street 20 B3
Dominick Place 21 B1
Dominick Street 38 A2-B2
Dominick Street, Lower 21 B1
Dominick Street, Upper 21 B1
Donaghmade Road 8 B2
Donard Road 25 B1
Donnybrook 28 B2
Donnybrook Road 28 B2 & 29 A2
Donnycarney Road 15 A1
Donore Avenue 21 A3
Donore Road 21 A3
Doonamana Road 47 B3
Doonanore Park 47 A3
Doonsalla Drive 47 A3
Doonsalla Park 47 A3
Doris Street 23 A3
Dorset Street, Lower 13 B3
Dorset Street, Upper 21 B1

Dowland Road 25 B2
Downpatrick Road 26 A1-B1
Dowth Avenue 13 A3
Drapier Road 4 B3
Drimnagh 25 B1
Drimnagh Road 25 B1
Dromard Road 25 B1
Dromawling Road 5 B3-6 A3
Dromore Road 26 A1
Drumcliffe Drive 12 B3
Drumcliffe Road 12 B3
Drumcondra 14 A2
Drumcondra Road, Lower 14 A2-A3
Drumcondra Road, Upper 14 A1
Drummartin Park 35 A3
Drummartin Road 35 A3
Drummartin Terrace 35 A2
Drury Street 21 B2
Dublin Street 9 B1
Dufferin Avenue 21 A3 & 27 A1
Duke Street 22 A2
Dundela Avenue 39 A3
Dundela Park 39 A3
Dundrum 34 A3
Dundrum Road 34 B1-B2
Dunedin Terrace 38 A3
Dún Laoghaire 38 B2 & 39 A2
Dunleary Hill 38 A2
Dunleary Road 38 A2
Dunluce Road 16 A2
Dunmanus Road 12 B2
Dunne Street 22 A1
Dunree Park 7 A2
Dunsink Park 1 A3-B3
Dunsink Lane 2 A3-B3
Dunville Avenue 28 A2
Durham Road 29 B1
Durrow Road 26 B2

E

EARL STREET, NORTH 22 A1
Earl Street, South 21 A2
Earlsfort Terrace 22 A3
East Road 23 A1
East Wall Road 14 B3 & 23 A2
Eaton Brae 34 A1
Eaton Place 37 B2
Eaton Road 27 A3
Eaton Square (Monkstown) 37 B2

Eaton Square
(Terenure) 27 A3
Eblana Avenue 38 B2
Eccles Street 13 B3
Echlin Street 21 A2
Eden Park 38 B3
Eden Park Avenue 35 A3
Eden Park Drive 35 A3
Eden Park Road 35 A3
Eden Quay 22 A2
Eden Road, Lower
38 B3 & 39 A3
Eden Road, Upper
38 B3 & 39 A3
Eden Terrace (Dún Laoghaire)
38 B3 & 39 A3
Eden Villas 38 B3 & 39 A3
Edenbrook Park 32 B3
Edenmore Avenue 7 B3
Edenmore Crescent 7 B3
Edenmore Drive 7 B3
Edenmore Gardens 7 B3
Edenmore Green 7 B3
Edenmore Grove 7 B3
Edenmore Park 7 B3
Edenmore Road 7 A2 & 8 A3
Edenvale Road 28 A2
Edmondstown 41 B2
Edmondstown Road 41 B2
Effra Road 27 B2
Eglinton Park
(Donnybrook) 28 B2
Eglinton Road 28 B2
Eglinton Terrace
(Dundrum) 34 B3
Elgin Road 28 B1
Ellenfield Road 5 B3
Ellesmere Avenue 12 B3 &
20 B1
Ellis Quay 21 A2
Elm Road 15 A1
Elm Mount Avenue 6 A3 &
15 A1
Elm Mount Park 6 A3
Elmwood Avenue, Lower
28 A1-A2
Elmwood Avenue, Upper
28 A1-A2
Elton Park 39 A3
Ely Place 22 A3
Ely Place, Upper 22 A3
Embassy Lawn 28 B3
Emmet Road 20 A3

Emmet Street
(N.C. Road) 14 A3
Emor Street 21 B3
Emorville Avenue 21 B3
Empress Place 22 A1
Ennafort Park 16 B1
Ennafort Road 16 B1
Erne Street, Lower 22 B2
Erne Street, Upper 22 B2
Errigal Road 25 B1
Erris Road 12 B3
Esmond Avenue 14 B3
Esposito Road 25 B2
Essex Quay 21 B2
Essex Street, East 21 B2
Eustace Street 21 B2
Exchequer Street 21 B2

F

FAIRFIELD ROAD 13 B2
Fairview Avenue, Lower 14
B3
Fairview Avenue, Upper 14
B2
Fairview Strand 14 B3
Fairy Hill 37 A3
Faith Avenue 14 B3
Faithche Bhaile an Déin 2 B3
Faithche Dhúin Since 3 A3
Faithche Measc 7 A3
Falcarragh Road 5 A3
Farmhill Drive 34 B2
Farmhill Park 34 B2 & 35 A2
Farmhill Road 34 B2 & 35 A2
Farney Park 23 A3-B3
Farnham Road 3 B3
Farrenboley Cottages 34 B1
Farrenboley Park 34 B1
Faughart Road 26 A2
Fassaugh Avenue 12 B2
Fassaugh Road 13 A3
Fergus Road 27 A3
Ferguson Road 14 A2
Ferndale Avenue 4 A3
Fernhill Park 31 B1
Fernhill Road 25 B3 & 31 B1
Ferns Road 26 B2
Ferrard Road 27 A3
Ferrycarrig Avenue 7 A1
Ferrycarrig Road 7 A1
Finglas 3 A3
Finglas Park 3 B2
Finglas Place 3 B3
Finglas Road 13 A1-B2

206

Glenageary Road, Lower   38
  B3
Glenageary Road, Upper, 38   A3
Glenalbyn Road   36   A3
Glenalua Road   48   A3
Glenart Avenue   36   B2
Glenarriff Road   11   B2
Glenaulin Drive   18   B1
Glenaulin Park   18   B1
Glenaulin Road   18   A1-A2
Glenavy Park   26   B3
Glenayle Road   7   B2
Glenbeigh Park   12   B3
Glenbeigh Road   12   B3 & 20
  B1
Glenbrook Road   11   B2
Glencloy Road   5   A3
Glencorp Road   5   B3
Glendale Park   32   A1
Glendhu Road   11   B2
Glendoher Drive   33   A3 & 42   A1
Glendoher Park   41   B1
Glendun Road   5   A3
Glendoher Avenue   33   A3
Glenealy Road   26   B1 & 27   A1
Glenfarne Road   7   B2
Glengarriff Parade   13   B3
Glenmalure Park   28   B3
Glenmaroon Park   8   A2
Glenmaroon Road   18   A1-A2
Glenomena Park   29   B3
Glenshesk Road   5   B3
Glentow Road   5   A3
Glenvar Park   36   B1
Glenwood Road   7   B3
Glin Avenue   6   B1
Glin Drive   6   B1
Glin Road   6   B1
Gloucester Street, South   22   A2
Goatstown Avenue   35   A2
Goatstown Road   35   A2
Goldenbridge Avenue   20   A3
Golden Lane   21   B3
Goldsmith Street   13   B3
Gordon Avenue   46   A2
Gordon Street   22   B3 & 23   A3
Gosworth Park   48   A1-B1
Gracefield   36   B2
Gracefield Road   7   A3
Grace Park Road   14   A2-B1
Grace Park Terrace   14   B2
Grafton Street   22   A2-A3
Granby Row   21   B1
Grand Canal Bank   20   B3

Grand Canal Quay   22   B2-B3
Grand Canal Street, Lower
  22   B3
Grand Canal Street, Upper
  22   B3
Grand Parade   28   A1
Grange Park (Baldoyle)   9   A1
Grange Park
  (Cornelscourt)   46   A1
Grange Park
  (Willbrook)   33   A3
Grange Park Estate
  (Raheny)   8   A3
Grange Park Avenue   8   A3
Grange Park Drive   8   A3
Grange Park Grove   8   A3
Grange Park Parade   8   A3
Grange Park Walk   8   A3
Grange Road
  (Raheny)   8   B1 & 9   A1
Grange Road
  (Rathfarnham)   33   A2-A3
Grangegorman, Lower   21   A1
Grangegorman, Upper   21   A1
Granitefield   47   A2
Grantham Place   21   B3
Grantham Street   21   B3
Granville Crescent   47   A3
Granville Park   46   A1
Granville Road
  (Cabinteely)   47   A3
Granville Road
  (Deans Grange)   46   A1
Grattan Crescent   19   B3
Grattan Street   22   B3
Greek Street   21   B2
Green Park   34   A1
Green Road
  (Blackrock)   36   B1-B2
Green Street   21   B1
Green Street, East   23   A2
Greencastle Avenue   7   A2
Greencastle Crescent   7   A2
Greencastle Drive   6   A1-A2
Greencastle Parade   7   A2
Greencastle Park   6   A1-A2
Greencastle Road   6   B1 & 7   A2
Greenfield Crescent   29   A3
Greenfield Park   29   A3
Greenfield Road (Mount
  Merrion)   35   B2 & 36   A2
Greenhill's Road   25   A3
Greenlea Avenue   26   B3
Greenlea Drive   26   B3

Greenlea Grove 26 B3
Greenlea Park 26 B3 & 32 B1
Greenlea Road 26 B3 & 32 B1
Greenmount Lane 27 A1
Greenmount Road 27 A3
Greentrees Park 25 B3
Greentrees Road 25 B3 &
 31 B1
Greenville Avenue 21 A3
Greenville Road 37 B2
Greenville Terrace 21 A3 &
 27 A1
Grenville Street 22 A1
Griffith Avenue 13 B1 & 15 A2
Griffith Drive 4 A3
Griffith Parade 4 A3
Grosvenor Place 27 B2
Grosvenor Road 27 B2
Grosvenor Square 27 B1-B2
Grotto Avenue 30 A3
Grotto Place 30 A3
Grove Avenue (Finglas) 3 B2
Grove Avenue (Mount Merrion)
 36 A2-B2
Grove Park (Rathmines) 27 B1
Grove Park Avenue 4 A2
Grove Park Crescent 4 A2
Grove Park Drive 4 A2
Grove Park Road 4 A2
Grove Road (Finglas) 3 B2
Grove Road
 (Rathmines) 27 B1
Guild Street 22 B1-B2
Gulistan Terrace 27 B1 &
 28 A1

H

HADDINGTON PARK
 48 A1
Haddington Road 22 B3
Haddon Road 15 B3
Haigh Terrace 38 B2
Hainault Park 46 A2
Hainault Road 46 A2-A3
Halliday Road 21 A1
Halston Street 21 B1-B2
Hammond Lane 21 A2
Hampstead Avenue 13 B1
Hanbury Lane 21 A2
Hannaville Park 27 A3
Hanover Quay 22 B3 & 23 A2
Hanover Street, East 22 B2
Harbour Road (Dalkey) 39 B3
Harcourt Street 21 B3

Hardebeck Avenue 25 B2
Hardiman Road 13 B1 & 14 **A2**
Hardwicke Street 21 B1
Harlech Crescent 35 A1
Harlech Grove 35 A1
Harmony Row 22 B2
Harold Road 21 A1
Harold's Cross 27 A1
Harold's Cross Road 27 A2
Harold's Grange Road 43 A2
Harrison Row 27 A3
Harty Avenue 25 B2
Harty Place 21 B3
Hatch Street, Lower 22 A3
Hatch Street, Upper 22 A3
Havelock Square 23 A3
Hawkins Street 22 A2
Hawthorn Lawn 10 A1
Hawthorn Terrace 22 A1
Hazel Avenue 35 B3
Hazel Road 15 A1
Hazel Villas 35 B3
Hazelbrook Drive 26 B3
Hazelbrook Road 26 B3
Hazelwood Drive 6 B3
Hazelwood Park 6 B3
Headford Grove 34 A2
Healthfield Road 27 A3
Heidelberg 35 A2
Hendrick Street 21 A2
Henly Park 34 A2
Henrietta Place 21 B1
Henrietta Street 21 B1
Henry Street 21 B1 & 22 **A1**
Herbert Avenue 29 B2
Herbert Park 28 B1
Herbert Place (Baggot Street,
 Lower) 22 B3
Herbert Road
 (Sandymount) 23 A3
Herbert Street 22 B3
Herberton Drive 26 B1
Herberton Road 20 B3 & 26 **B1**
Heytesbury Lane 28 B1
Heytesbury Street 28 B3
High Street 21 B2
Highfield Grove 27 B3
Highfield Park 34 A1 B1
Highfield Road 27 B3
Highridge Green 35 B3
Highthorn Park 38 A3
Hill Street 22 A1
Hillcourt Road 47 A1
Hillcrest Road 44 A3-B2

Hillsbrook Avenue   25   B3 & 26   A3
Hillsbrook Drive   26   A3
Hillsbrook Grove   25   B3
Hillside   48   B1
Hillside Drive   33   B1-B2
Hillside Park   32   B3
Hogan Place   22   B2
Holles Street   22   B3
Holly Park Avenue   37   A3
Holly Road   15   A1
Hollybank Avenue, Lower   28   B2
Hollybank Avenue, Upper   28   B2
Hollybank Road   14   A2
Hollybrook Grove   15   A2
Hollybrook Park   15   B2
Hollybrook Road   15   B2-B3
Hollywood Drive   35   A2
Holmston Avenue   38   B3
Home Farm Park   14   A2
Home Farm Road   13   B1 & 14   A1
Hope Avenue   14   B3
Horton Court   27   A3
Howth Road   8   B3 & 15   A3
Huband Road   25   A1
Hudson Road   39   A3
Hughes Road, East   25   B2
Hughes Road, North   25   B2
Hughes Road, South   25   B2
Hume Street   22   A3
Hyde Park (Dalkey)   39   A3
Hyde Park (Templeogue)   32   B1
Hyde Park Avenue   36   B1-B2
Hyde Road   39   B3

I

IDRONE TERRACE   37   A1
Imaal Road   13   A3
Inagh Road   18   A3
Inchicore   19   B3
Inchicore Road   19   B3 & 20   A3
Inchicore Square   19   B3
Inchicore Terrace, North   19   B3
Inchicore Terrace, South   19   B3
Infirmary Road   20   B1-B2
Innisfallen Parade   13   B3
Innishmaan Road   5   A3
Inns Quay   21   B2
Inver Road   12   B2-B3

Inverness Road   14   B2
Iona Crescent   13   B2
Iona Drive   13   B2
Iona Park   13   B2
Iona Road   13   B2
Iona Villas   13   B2
Iris Grove   35   B1
Irishtown   23   B2
Irishtown Road   23   A2-A3
Irvine Terrace   22   B1
Islandbridge   20   A2
Island Street   21   A2
Ivar Street   21   A1
Iveagh Gardens   26   A1
Iveleary Road   5   A3
Iveragh Road   5   A3

J

JAMES   LARKIN   ROAD   17   B1
James's Place, East   22   B3
James's Street, East   22   B3
Jamestown Avenue   19   A3-B3
Jamestown Road (Finglas)   3   B1 & 3   B3
Jamestown Road (Inchicore)   19   A3-B3
Jane Place, Lower   22   B1
Jervis Street   21   B1-B2
John Dillon Street   21   B2
John MacCormack Avenue   25   B2
John Street, South   21   A3
John Street, West   21   A2
Johnstown Avenue   47   A2
Johnstown Grove   47   A2
Johnstown Park   47   A2
Johnstown Road   47   A2-A3
Jones's Road   14   A3
Joyce Avenue   46   A3
Joyce Road   13   B2 & 14   A2

K

KEEPER ROAD   26   A1-B1
Kells Road   26   B2
Kelly's Avenue   38   B2
Kenilworth Park   27   A2
Kenilworth Road   27   B2
Kenilworth Square   27   B2
Keogh Square   19   B3
Kerrymount Rise   46   A3
Kevin Street, Cross   21   B3
Kevin Street, Lower   21   B3
Kevin Street, Upper   21   B3
Kickham Road   20   A3

Military Road (Rathmines) 27 B1
Mill Lane (Palmerston) 18 A1
Mill Street 21 A3
Millbourne Avenue 14 A2
Millgate Drive 31 B1
Millmount Avenue 14 A2
Milltown 28 B3
Milltown Bridge Road 28 B3
Milltown Drive 34 A1
Milltown Park 28 B2
Milltown Road 28 A3-B2
Misery Hill 22 B2
Moatfield Avenue 7 A3
Moatfield Park 7 A3
Moatfield Road 7 A3
Moeran Road 25 B2
Molesworth Street 22 A2
Monaloe Avenue 47 A2
Monaloe Drive 47 A2
Monaloe Park Road 46 B2 & 47 A2
Monaloe Way 47 A2
Monasterboice Road 26 A2-B2
Monck Place 13 A3-B3
Monkstown 37 B2
Monkstown Avenue 37 B3
Monkstown Crescent 38 A2
Monkstown Farm 37 B3
Monkstown Road 37 B2
Montague Street 21 B3
Montpelier Hill 20 B2
Montpelier Parade 37 B2
Montrose Crescent 6 B3
Montrose Drive 6 A2
Moore Street 21 B1
Morehampton Road 28 B1
Morehampton Terrace 28 B1
Mornington Road 28 A2
Moss Street 22 A2
Mount Albion 34 A3
Mount Anville Road 35 A2-B2
Mount Argus Road 27 A2
Mount Brown 20 B2
Mount Carmel Avenue 34 B2
Mount Carmel Park 31 B3
Mount Carmel Road 34 B2
Mount Drummond Avenue 27 B1
Mount Drummond Square 27 B1
Mount Eden Road 28 B2
Mount Merrion 35 B2

Mount Merrion Avenue 36 A2-B1
Mount Prospect Avenue 16 A2 & 17 A2
Mount Prospect Drive 16 B2
Mount Prospect Grove 16 B2
Mount Prospect Park 16 B2
Mount Salus Road 49 A1-A2
Mount Street, Lower 22 B3
Mount Street, Upper 22 B3
Mount Tallant Avenue 27 A3
Mount Temple Road 21 A1
Mount Town, Lower 38 A3
Mount Town, Upper 38 A3
Mountainview Road 28 A2
Mountdown Park 31 B1
Mountdown Road 31 B1
Mountjoy Square 22 A1
Mountjoy Street 21 B1
Mount Pleasant Avenue, Lower 27 B1 & 28 A1
Mount Pleasant Avenue, Upper 27 B1 & 28 A1
Mount Prospect Avenue 16 B1 & 17 A2
Mountshannon Road 20 B3
Mount Wood 38 A3
Mourne Road 20 A3 & 26 A1
Moycullen Road 18 A3
Moyle Road 12 B2
Moyne Road 28 A2
Muckross Avenue 25 B3 & 26 A3
Muckross Green 26 A3
Mulgrave Street 38 B2
Mulgrave Terrace 38 B3
Mulroy Road 12 B2
Mulvey Park 34 B1
Munster Street 13 A3-B3
Murphystown Road 44 B2
Muskerry Road 18 B3 & 19 A3
Myrtle Grove 36 A3
Myrtle Park 38 B3

N

NAAS ROAD 25 A1-B1
Nash Street 19 A3-B3
Nassau Street 22 A2
Navan Road 10 A1 & 12 B3
Neagh Road 26 B3
Nelson Street 13 B3
Nephin Road 12 A2-A3
Nerano Road 49 A1
Neville Road 27 B3

216

Plunkett Crescent   3   A2
Plunkett Drive   3   A2
Plunkett Green   3   A2
Plunkett Grove   3   A2
Plunkett Road   3   A2
Poddle Park   26   B3
Poolbeg Street   22   A2
Poplar Row   14   B3
Portland Place   14   A3
Portland Row   22   A1
Portland Street, North   14   A3
Portland Street, West   21   A2
Portobello Road   27   B1
Pottery Road   46   B1 & 47   A2
Prebend Street   21   B1
Prince's Lane   (Ranelagh)   28   A1
Priory Avenue   36   A2
Priory Drive   36   A2
Priory Grove   36   A2
Priory Road   27   A2
Proby Square   37   A2
Prospect Avenue   13   B2
Prospect Road   13   B3
Prussia Street   21   A1

Q

QUARRY COTTAGES   25   B3
Quarry Road   12   B3
Queen's Park   37   B2
Queen's Road   38   B2
Queen's Street   21   A2
Queen's Terrace   22   B2
Quinn's Lane   22   A3

R

RAFTER'S LANE   26   A1
Rafter's Road   26   A1
Raglan Lane   28   B1
Raglan Road   28   B1
Raheny   17   A1
Raheny Park   17   A1
Railway Avenue (Inchicore)   19   A3-B3
Railway Street   22   A1
Rainsford Street   21   A2
Raleigh Square   26   A1
Ramillies Road   18   B3 & 19   A3
Ramleh Park   28   B3
Ranelagh   28   A1
Ranelagh Road   28   A1-A2
Raon Naomh Áine   17   A1
Raon an Mhuilinn   16   B1 & 17   A1

Raphoe Road   26   A1
Rathdown Avenue   33   A1
Rathdown Crescent   33   A1
Rathdown Drive   32   B1 & 33   A1
Rathdown Park   33   A1
Rathdown Road   13   A3
Rathdown Villas   33   A1
Rathfarnham   32   A2
Rathfarnham Park   33   A1
Rathfarnham Road   32   A1-A2
Rathgar   27   B3
Rathgar Avenue   27   A2-B3
Rathgar Road   27   B2-B3
Rathland Road   26   B3
Rathlin Road   13   B1
Rathmines   27   B2 & 28   A2
Rathmines Road, Lower   27   B1
Rathmines Road, Upper   27   B2
Rathmore Avenue   35   B3
Rathmore Park   8   A3
Ratoath Road   2   B3 & 12   B3
Ratra Road   11   B2
Ravensdale Park   26   B3
Ravensdale Road   23   A1
Redesdale Road   35   B2-B3
Réidh Loreto   33   B3
Reuben Avenue   20   B3
Reuben Street   20   B3
Rialto Street   20   B3
Richmond Avenue (Monkstown)   37   B2
Richmond Avenue, North   14   B3
Richmond Avenue, South   28   A3
Richmond Grove   37   B3
Richmond Hill (Rathmines)   27   B1
Richmond Hill (Monkstown)   38   A2
Richmond Road   14   A2-B3
Richmond Street, North   14   A3
Richmond Street, South   27   B1
Richview Park   28   A3
Ring Street   19   B3
Ringsend   23   A2
Ringsend Park   23   A2-B2
Ringsend Road   22   B2 & 23   A2
River Road   1   A3 & 11   B1
Riversdale Avenue   33   A1
Riverside Avenue   6   B1
Riverside Drive   6   B1
Riverside Grove   6   B1
Riverside Road   6   B1

217

218

St Kevin's Gardens 27 B3
St Kevin's Park (Rathgar) 27 B3
St Kevin's Park (Stillorgan) 35 B3
St Kevin's Villas 47 B1
St Killian's Avenue 25 A3
St Laurence Road (Ballyfermot) 19 A2
St Laurence Park 36 A2-A3
St Lawrence Road (Clontarf) 15 B2-B3
St Malachy's Drive 25 A3
St Margaret's Road 3 A1
St Martin's Park 26 B2
St Mary's Avenue, West 19 B2
St Mary's Crescent 25 B2
St Mary's Drive 25 B2
St Mary's Park 25 B2
St Mary's Road, North (East Wall) 22 B1
St Mary's Road, South (Ballsbridge) 22 B3
St Mary's Road (Crumlin) 25 B2
St Mel's Avenue 31 A1
St Nicholas Place 16 B2
St Pappin Road 4 B3
St Patrick's Crescent 38 A3
St Patrick's Cottages 33 A3
St Patrick's Road (Dalkey) 48 B1
St Patrick's Road (Walkinstown) 25 B3
St Patrick's Terrace (Inchicore) 19 B3
St Peter's Crescent 25 B3
St Peter's Drive 25 B3
St Peter's Road (Phibsborough) 13 A3
St Peter's Road (Walkinstown) 25 B3
St Stephen's Green, East 22 A3
St Stephen's Green, North 22 A3
St Stephen's Green, South 22 A3
St Stephen's Green, West 22 A3
St Teresa's Road (Crumlin) 26 A2-A3
St Thomas Road (Ardee Street) 21 A3
St Thomas' Road (Mount Merrion) 35 B1

St Vincent's Park 37 A2
St Vincent Street, West 19 B3
Salamanca 35 A2
Sallymount Avenue 28 A1
Sallynoggin 47 B1
Sallynoggin Park 47 A1
Sallynoggin Road 47 A1-B1
Salzburg 35 A2
Sandford Avenue (Donnybrook) 28 B2
Sandford Avenue (Donore Avenue) 21 A3
Sandford Road 28 B2
Sandwith Street, Lower 22 B2
Sandwith Street, Upper 22 B2
Sandycove Avenue, East 39 A3
Sandycove Avenue, North 39 A3
Sandycove Avenue, West 39 A3
Sandycove Point 39 A3
Sandycove Road 39 A3
Sandyford 44 A2
Sandyford Road 34 B3 & 44 A2
Sandymount 29 B1
Sandymount Avenue 29 A1-B1
Sandymount Road 23 B3
Sans Souci Park 36 A1
Santry 5 B2
Santry Avenue 5 A1
Santry Close 5 B1
Santry Villas 5 B2
Sarah Curran Road 33 A3
Sarsfield Street (Sallynoggin) 47 B1
Sarto Road 9 A3
Saul Road 26 B1
Saval Grove 48 A1
Saval Park Gardens 48 A1
Saval Park Road 48 A1
Scholarstown Road 41 A2
Seafield Avenue (Clontarf) 16 B2
Seafield Avenue (Monkstown) 37 B2
Seafield Close 29 B3
Seafield Crescent 30 A3
Seafield Road, East 16 B3
Seafield Road, West 16 A3
Seafield Road (Booterstown) 29 B3
Seafort Avenue 23 B3
Seafort Gardens 23 B3

Seán Mac Dermott Street, Lower 22 A1
Seán Mac Dermott Street, Upper 22 A1
Seapark Drive 16 B3
Seapark Road 16 B2-B3
Seapoint Avenue 37 B1-B2
Seaview Avenue, East 14 B3 & 22 B1
Seaview Avenue, North 15 B3
Seaview Terrace (Donnybrook) 29 A2
Serpentine Avenue 29 A1
Serpentine Park 23 A3
Serpentine Road 23 A3
Seville Place 22 B1
Shamrock Villas 27 A2
Shanboley Road 5 B3
Shandon Crescent 13 A3
Shandon Drive 13 A3
Shandon Park Gardens 13 A2
Shandon Park (Monkstown) 37 B2
Shandon Park (Phibsborough) 13 A3
Shandon Road 13 A3
Shangan Avenue 5 A2
Shangan Gardens 5 A2
Shangan Road 4 B2 & 5 A2
Shanglas Road 5 B3
Shanid Road 27 A2
Shanliss Avenue 5 A2
Shanliss Drive 5 A2
Shanliss Grove 5 A2
Shanliss Park 5 A2
Shanliss Road 5 A2
Shanliss Walk 5 A2
Shanliss Way 5 A2
Shanowen Avenue 5 A3
Shanowen Drive 5 A3
Shanowen Grove 4 B3 & 5 A3
Shanowen Road 5 A3
Shanrath Road 5 B2-B3
Shantalla Avenue 5 B3
Shantalla Park 5 B3
Shantalla Road 5 B3
Shanvarna Road 5 B2-B3
Shelbourne Road 23 A3
Shelmalier Road 22 B1-A1
Shelmartin Avenue 14 B2
Shelton Drive 26 A1
Shelton Gardens 26 A1
Shelton Grove 26 A1

Shelton Park 26 A1
Sheriff Street, Lower 22 B1
Sheriff Street, Upper 23 A1
Sherrard Street, Lower 14 A3
Sherrard Street, Upper 14 A3
Ship Street, Great 21 B2
Ship Street, Little 21 B2
Shrewsbury Park 29 B1
Shrewsbury Road 29 A2
Silchester Crescent 38 B3
Silchester Park 38 B3 & 47 B1
Silchester Road 38 B3
Silloge Avenue 4 B2
Silloge Gardens 4 B2
Silloge Road 4 A2-B2
Silver Birches 35 A3
Silverwood Drive 32 B2
Silverwood Road 32 B2
Simmonscourt Road 29 A1
Sion Hill Avenue 27 A2
Sion Hill Road 14 B1
Sion Road 47 B1
Sir John Rogerson's Quay 22 B2
Sitric Road 21 A1
Skelly's Lane 6 A3
Skreen Road 12 A3
Slane Road 26 B1
Slemish Road 12 A3
Slievebloom Park 25 B1-B2
Slievebloom Road 25 B1-B2
Slievemore Road 26 A1
Slievenamon Road 20 A3 & 26 A1
Slieve Rua Drive 35 B3
Sloperton 38 A2
Smithfield 21 A2
Somerville Avenue 25 B2
Sorrento Road 49 A1
South Avenue 35 B2
South Circular Road (Dolphin's Barn) 20 B3
South Circular Road (Kilmainham) 20 A3
South Circular Road (Portobello) 27 B1
South Dock Street 23 A2
South Great George's Street 21 B2
South Hill 28 A3
South Hill Avenue 36 A1
South Hill Park 36 A1
South Lotts Road 23 A2-A3

220

221

222